HOW TO STORE YOUR
GARDEN PRODUCE

How to Store Your Garden Produce

The key to self-sufficiency

Piers Warren

Revised and enlarged edition

with illustrations by Tessa Pettingell

green books

This revised and enlarged edition
first published in 2008
by Green Books Ltd
Foxhole, Dartington
Totnes, Devon TQ9 6EB

Reprinted 2008 (twice), 2009

Text printed on 100% post-consumer waste paper
by TJ International Ltd, Padstow, Cornwall, UK

ISBN 978 1 900322 17 1

Contents

Contents (continued)

Introduction

Why is storing your garden produce the key to self-sufficiency?

Because with less than an acre of garden you can grow enough produce to feed a family of four for a year, but since much of the produce will become ready at the same time – in the summer and autumn – most of it will go to waste without proper storage, and you'll be off to the supermarket again.

I've always been obsessed with the idea of self-sufficiency, and have always hated waste, so as a keen vegetable grower it was only natural that I explored the overlooked art of storage. To some extent it is a lost art. These days you can go to the supermarket any day of the week and buy produce from many different countries. Imagine being told that the lettuces were all sold out – try again in six months! In the past, effective storage was a matter of life and death: if your potatoes rotted, your family would go hungry – possibly starve.

I have also always felt ridiculous buying vegetables or fruit that have been flown halfway round the world when I had been growing a surplus of the same ones myself only a few months earlier.

Plus there are so many other benefits from eating your own produce year round:

1. A huge sense of satisfaction – of self-reliance – that you alone can meet the most important need of your family.

2. Home-grown fruit and vegetables are far cheaper than shop-bought (if not free) – and you will have healthy exercise growing them. Why pay expensive gym fees and work out in a sweaty windowless room

when the Green Gym is right outside your own back door, or down on the allotment? It is also said that gardeners live longer because they are always looking forward to the next season – of growing, harvesting and storing.

3. What are you eating? You have little chance of knowing what chemicals or genetic modification have been used on produce you buy from a shop. At least you know how your own fruit and veg have been raised – and if you're an organic gardener like me (which I thoroughly recommend), you'll know your produce couldn't be safer, for both you and the environment.

4. Eating food you have produced in your own garden is by far the most environmentally sound way of doing things: no unnecessary packaging, no transport pollution, no encouragement of vast monocrops and so on.

5. You can create your own by-products: storage may simply be a result of your desire to create a specific product or ingredient such as cider or dried mushrooms.

6. Pleasure! Some storage activities: stringing onions, making wine, concocting chutneys, are pleasurable in themselves – and the end products are definitely for enjoyment.

Why do you need special methods in the first place?

When keeping fresh food for any length of time you have four main enemies: enzymes, bacteria, yeasts and fungi.

Enzymes are proteins naturally found in all fresh produce which control various processes; some of them help break down food as we digest it. They can work pretty quickly: for example, they are responsible for apples turning rapidly brown when cut. Enzymes can spoil food soon after harvesting, so our aim must be to halt their action as quickly as possible. Extreme heat stops the enzymes working permanently, as is the case in bottling. Extreme cold (–18°C / –1°F or less) stops them working temporarily, as in freezing.

Bacteria are micro-organisms which can multiply rapidly. They are the main causes of food poisoning, either by producing toxins (e.g. causing botulism), or by being poisonous themselves. Contamination can come from anywhere: soil, hands, utensils, apparently clean jars etc., so the key is to halt or slow their growth. This can be done by killing them with extreme heat, or slowing their activity with cold, a high concentration of sugar or salt, or acid conditions – as in pickling.

(Note that preventing botulism is discussed in more detailed in the section on Bottling on page 23).

Yeasts are also microscopic, but are not dangerous like bacteria and of course they can be our allies when fermenting sugar to make cider, wine and beer. In terms of spoilage they are most often responsible for fermenting jams; and as yeasts are destroyed by heat, this means they contaminate the jam after potting. Their activity is slowed down by cold, which is why it is a good idea to keep opened jars of jam in the fridge.

Fungi produce minuscule spores that are in the air all around us, so any uncovered food will sooner or later be infected. As the fungal growth develops, the food will appear mouldy and will be unfit for consumption – although rarely dangerous. Freezing, pickling etc. will stop fungal growth, but equally important are methods to stop spores reaching the food in the first place: burying harvested carrots in sand, for example.

Storage and preservation techniques fight these enemies mainly by using heat, cold or acid, by removing moisture, or simply by creating conditions where spoilage is less likely.

Note that although there are some methods – such as drying and bottling – that may render food safe to eat for many years, your aim should be to store food only until the next season's fresh produce is available (perhaps an exception to this is some wines which can improve with age to a certain point). This ensures you are eating the highest quality stored food at all times. There is no point in eating tough old broad beans that have sat in the freezer for many months when you have pods bursting with succulent fresh beans in the garden. So, planning quantities and timing is essential for good storage.

So how can this book help you?

Part One looks at the various storage methods in general. Many of these are applicable to a range of produce. Start here to get a good background of the methods available. It is true that some of the methods would be more accurately defined as preservation rather than storage (making jam for example), but the idea is to have the full range of possibilities in front of you when deciding what to do with your mountain of raspberries.

Part Two is more of a reference section, which lists most plant produce grown commonly in gardens and allotments. For each one, the most appropriate methods are listed with specific advice. Your choice of method will depend on various factors, including quantity of produce to be stored, equipment and space available, family tastes, and personal preferences. You may have grown gherkins specifically for pickling, for example, or extra strawberries for jam-making.

Each section in Part Two also contains a list of recommended varieties. Where possible these have been chosen because they are varieties particularly suitable for storage; otherwise they are personal favourites or unusual varieties worth trying.

Some methods, such as the clamping of roots, have been passed through many generations. Others, such as freezing, are relatively new. And there are those which are continually developing: invent a new chutney for example, and you have added to the armoury of storage methods.

Part One

The Methods

GENERAL GUIDELINES

1. Harvest produce for storage in its peak condition.

2. Handle produce carefully – bruised fruit and vegetables will rot quickly.

3. If you have to process your produce in some way before storage (e.g. the freezing of peas) do this immediately after harvesting, as enzymes can get to work very quickly and reduce the quality of the product.

4. Some varieties store better than others – if you are growing some crops for storage, research your varieties first.

5. Do not store near strong-smelling substances or hazardous chemicals – often a problem when storing in a garage or garden shed. Creosote-flavoured potatoes are not my favourite.

6. Always label any stored produce with a description of contents and the date of preserving or storing.

7. Check your stored produce regularly – remove any that is rotting to reduce the chance of it spreading.

8. Plan what you store (and therefore grow) according to your family's tastes. There's little point in storing twenty pumpkins if your family is bored with eating them after two or three.

9. The priority should always be to EAT the freshest produce while fresh, then store the excess. If you have a freezer full of year-old broccoli, you have simply grown too much broccoli.

10. As well as storage techniques, extend your growing season, if you can, using a greenhouse, polytunnel and/or cold-frames. You will be eating fresh produce for longer, and can grow a wider range of varieties.

BASIC STORAGE

In some cases the very simplest form of storage is to leave it to nature. Various crops, like leeks for example, can be left in the ground until required. I have often harvested perfectly good leeks in May that were sown twelve months earlier. Of course the vegetable has to be frost-hardy to survive the winter, so in many other cases it is better to harvest the produce when it is in peak condition and place it in an environment where long-term storage is possible. Often this means a location which is cool but frost-free. For many years cellars have been used for this purpose, and in some countries it is common to have a 'root-cellar' specifically built with storage in mind. People without cellars, especially in modern urban houses, will have to resort to sheds and garages which, although not ideal, can be perfectly adequate.

Potatoes, for example, can be stored for long periods in a cool, dark location, in paper, hessian or cotton sacks, or even cardboard boxes. Humidity needs to be low to deter fungal growth, which is why they should not be stored in plastic bags for any period of time. The problem with a small garden shed is that it will warm up in the spring and the tubers may start to sprout roots and shoots, so a cooler brick or stone outbuilding will enable longer storage. A really hard frost may freeze a wooden shed and all its contents solid – thereby spoiling any produce stored within when it thaws.

Fruits such as apples and pears can be stored on shelves or in boxes. They need a slightly different environment in that they like the air to be a little moist. A cool dark outhouse is ideal – you can occasionally wet the floor to keep the humidity up. Choose only perfect unblemished specimens for dry storage. The fruit should not be touching, so either space them apart or wrap individually in paper – this stops the rotting fungi and bacteria spreading from one to another. Greaseproof paper is good, but even newspaper is better than nothing. If you have hundreds of apples you may not have the patience for wrapping each one, so why not just wrap a few crates-worth for the longest storage – you should still be eating them next spring. Note that the fruit that ripens late in the season will keep better, and some varieties, such as Cox and Bramley, keep better than others.

When produce is stored short-term in the kitchen, it helps if you use a receptacle that allows plenty of ventilation in order to decrease the humidity and therefore the likelihood of rotting due to fungal growths. You can buy special fruit bowls with holes around the bottom, wire baskets, or even use a colander. It's also a good idea to store bananas separately from other fruits as when they are yellow they are already at an advanced stage of ripeness and release a gas called ethylene which encourages surrounding fruit to ripen faster. 'Banana trees' (usually a metal hook on a stand) are a stylish way of hanging a bunch of bananas, and you could then position this at the opposite end of the kitchen from your fruit bowl or even in a different room.

In general, produce which traditionally grows and ripens in a warm environment will store better in the average kitchen than in the fridge. Bananas (which are of course from the tropics), for example, quickly go black if stored in the fridge, and tomatoes (which originated in the warm deserts of South America) will ripen properly and keep a better flavour on the kitchen surface rather than when refrigerated. Incidentally, while we're talking of tomatoes and bananas, if you have picked a number of tomatoes which haven't ripened fully (at the end of the season for example) and you want to speed the process up, you can put them in a jar or bag with a ripe banana in a warm room and the ethylene produced will help speed the tomatoes along.

Hanging is a simple technique mainly used for onions and squashes. The best place to hang vegetables for storage is in a dry cool airy place which won't be hit by hard frosts. A stone or brick outbuilding is ideal as long as it isn't too damp. A garage might suffice as long as it doesn't smell of petrol or oil, but certainly not the warm kitchen – no matter how attractive strings of onions may look.

Squashes such as marrows and pumpkins can be hung in nets – just make sure the fruits are not touching each other. Save any netting or net bags for this purpose: such as the net sacks that stock-feed carrots often come in. Netting bags (or even tights) can be used for hanging onions or garlic, but just aren't as picturesque as stringing. Instructions on how to create a string can be found in the Onions section in Part Two, page 97.

Some roots, such as carrots, parsnips and beetroots, can be stored in sand or sawdust (or a peat substitute). The important points are:

1. Use sand that is only just moist – if too wet, prepare in advance by spreading out your sand on a plastic sheet in the hot sun in the summer, then keep in plastic sacks under cover until needed.

2. Make layers of sand and roots (unwashed but with excess soil gently brushed off) in containers such as barrels, crates, deep seed trays – making sure the roots don't touch each other.

3. Store the containers in a dry, frost-free place. If they are large, fill them *in situ* (have you ever tried to lift a barrel full of sand?).

CLAMPING

Clamping is a simple method for storing a large quantity of root vegetables outside. It's a useful technique where indoor storage space is limited, but not so good if you have very hard frosts. Basically it is a pile of roots with straw and earth on top. The following guidelines will help your clamped roots store longer:

1. Choose a site on a piece of ground unlikely to become waterlogged.

2. Harvest your root crops and allow them to dry on the surface of the soil for a couple of hours.

3. To build the clamp, start with a good layer of straw or bracken, and on top of this pile up your potatoes or other roots in a pyramid shape.

4. Cover the pile with a layer of straw or bracken and leave to sweat for a day or two (the evaporation of excess moisture).

5. Then cover the straw with a layer of fairly dry earth about 15cm / 6 inches thick – making sure there are a few small tunnels of straw sticking through the earth along the bottom and chimneys along the top to allow for air circulation. Pat the earth flat with a spade to form a smooth, steep-sided pyramid that rain will easily run off.

Make a series of smaller clamps rather than one enormous one – when you want a handful of potatoes it's not easy to burrow into a clamp and then rebuild it. It's better to dismantle a small clamp and bring a sackful of spuds into a shed or garage for easy access until the next clamp is needed.

FREEZING

Freezing is a method that has relatively recently revolutionised the storage of fruit and vegetables for many households. It's also quick, easy, and very effective.

Freezing halts, or at least dramatically slows down, the action of enzymes (which break down vitamins, for example) which occurs from the moment food is harvested. So food frozen shortly after picking will be among the healthiest of stored produce. The cold also stops microorganisms from growing and spreading. Many fruit and vegetables can be stored in a deep-freezer for up to twelve months – giving you year-round access to home-grown goodness. As already mentioned, you should never need to keep anything longer than a year, so if frozen produce gets this old, discard it and replace with smaller quantities of freshly harvested crops.

If you are serious about storage you will soon find you need a chest freezer (or two!). For the average home, the ideal combination would be to have an upright fridge-freezer in the kitchen, where you can store small amounts for quick access, and then a chest (or upright) freezer in a garage, utility room etc., for the bulk of your frozen produce.

A few general rules

1. Freeze food as quickly as possible after harvesting: some produce, like peas and sweetcorn for example, will start to lose its sweetness within minutes of being picked. Timing is everything.

2. Freeze your best. If you don't like tough, stringy beans, you won't like them after they've been frozen either. Freeze young and tender and perfect – not forgetting to EAT as much fresh as you want first, of course.

3. Pack food in appropriate plastic bags or containers. This is partly to exclude as much air as possible, since air dries out the food and slows freezing. Save old ice-cream containers, margarine tubs and yoghurt pots for use in the freezer.

4. Label your packages. What is that bag of green mush that's been sitting there for a year?! It's best to write on the bag or container with a waterproof pen – mentioning what it is and, importantly, the date of freezing.

5. When food is frozen after blanching (or cooking) make sure it is completely cool before putting it in the freezer.

6. Do not place unfrozen food against deep-frozen packages – they will start to thaw and the frozen food will deteriorate. Some freezers have a rack at the top for placing the new food on as it freezes.

7. If you are freezing liquids such as fruit juices, remember they will expand as they freeze. So freeze in plastic bags inside old drinks cartons – once frozen, the blocks can be stacked with no wastage of space. Or freeze in empty (and well-cleaned) plastic milk containers – but leave a space at the top for expansion.

8. Some freezers have a fast-freeze button which overrides the thermostat and keeps the temperature low while new additions are freezing. Don't forget to switch this off after a few hours (depending on the amount of unfrozen food added). The freezer will then return to the normal temperature of –18°C (–1°F) or so.

9. Organise your freezer. You may find coloured bags or boxes help you find the right items quickly. Rotate your stock: a three year-old bag of sprouts that you will never eat is a waste of space. You might even find it useful to keep a list of what is in the freezer with dates, and then cross items off as you use them.

10. Cook (or eat) food as soon as possible after it comes out of the freezer, as the spoiling enzymes will start working again straight away (as well as any bacteria or fungi that may have contaminated the food). Vegetables can generally best be cooked from frozen, while fruits are better left to thaw slowly in the fridge.

Open-freezing

Some fruit and vegetables (e.g. broccoli) stick together in a lump when frozen, making it difficult to remove small portions later without smashing the lump to green shrapnel.

The solution is 'open-freezing': simply lay the food out on a baking sheet so that the individual pieces are not touching, and place this in the freezer. When frozen, the food can be placed in a bag or container to exclude as much air as possible. Now when you come to use the frozen food it should be suitably loose. Some freezers have a pull-out tray in the top specifically for this purpose.

Blanching

Recommended for nearly all vegetables, blanching is the immersing of the fresh produce in boiling water for a minute or two immediately before freezing. The reason for doing this is to slow down the enzymes which cause the food to deteriorate – even while frozen. This improves the colour, flavour and nutritional value of the food.

As a rule of thumb, blanch small pieces of vegetables (e.g. peas, beans) for one minute, and larger pieces (e.g. cauliflower, parsnips) for two minutes. A few vegetables need longer blanching and these are detailed in Part Two.

Usually I find I am blanching fairly large quantities of harvested crops at the same time. The best method I have found is:

- Use two large pans: one filled with water and brought to the boil.

- In the sink, have a large bowl or two of cold water ready (adding lumps of ice from the freezer will help).

- Place the first batch of vegetables (say 500g / 1lb 2 oz) in the hot water, bring back to the boil and then time for the relevant number of minutes.

- Carefully pour through a colander into the second pan, and put that on the hot plate in place of the first.

- Tip the vegetables from the colander into a bowl of cold water and swirl around to cool quickly.

- When the water (in the second pan) returns to the boil, add the next batch of vegetables, boil and time as before.

- While this is happening, tip the first batch of vegetables in the cold water through another colander and refill the bowl with cold water ready to cool the next lot (or leave for several batches if still icy). You may find a wire basket – such as a chip basket – useful for dipping the food into the pan and the cold water without the need for tipping.

After a while you will develop a good routine for this. The main things to be careful with are not to boil the vegetables for too long, to cool them quickly after blanching, and to ensure they are completely cool before bagging and freezing.

Cooked Produce

Some fruit and vegetables can be frozen after they have been cooked – for example new potatoes, tomato purée, stewed apples or plums. Some are detailed in Part Two where relevant, but of course it's common sense that many cooked dishes can be frozen for later use – another form of produce storage.

Defrosting the freezer

The best time to do this is in the spring, as the freezer should be at its emptiest, having been raided all winter.

First, empty the contents (throwing away anything too old or unwanted on the compost heap) and make a pile of the frozen food in cool boxes or on newspaper on the floor. Cover this pile with paper, towels, blankets – anything to insulate it.

Switch the freezer off, place a wad of newspaper inside, in the bottom, and a large pan of hot water on top of the paper. Close the lid and leave for thirty minutes. This may be long enough, but if there is still a lot of ice inside put in a fresh pan of hot water and leave for another twenty minutes or so.

When all the ice has gone, soak up the water and give the freezer a good clean inside. Then close the lid, switch on, and after fifteen minutes replace the food.

DRYING

Enzymes, bacteria, yeasts and fungi all require moisture, so drying food is effective at preventing the action of all of them. Well-dried produce has a long storage life and often an intensified flavour, so this technique is often used to create desired ingredients such as dried mushrooms, chillies or tomatoes, or goodies to be eaten direct such as dried apple rings (home-dried fruit can be a healthy and tasty addition to packed lunches for school or work).

The choice of whether to dry, freeze or use some other technique may depend on your intended future use for the produce. Beans, peas and sweetcorn used to be dried every autumn by many country families for winter use, but a pea freshly cooked from the freezer will be more tender and flavoursome and will contain more vitamins. On the other hand, dried produce weighs far less than when hydrated, and so is popular with backpackers and in situations where weight is a factor. In addition, glass jars of dried fruits and mushrooms and strings of dried chillies can look extremely attractive in the kitchen and make unusual presents.

A warm, dry place is needed for drying. An airing cupboard may do but will take a few days – a warm oven (45°-55°C/ 110°-130° F) will take a few hours. Herbs can be hung in bunches or laid out on a baking sheet. Apples can also be dried by slicing thinly – threading on a string – and hanging over the stove or warmed gently in an oven for a few hours. Once dried, the produce must be stored in airtight jars.

Beans and peas are best dried by leaving the pods on the plants until they have turned yellow; then cut the plant at ground level and hang indoors to dry completely. When the pods have become brittle, shell them and leave on trays for a few more days. Then store in a cool dry place in airtight containers.

If you want to take the drying of produce a step further, other options include using home-made drying boxes, solar dryers or food dehydrators.

A drying box can be made simply out of a large wooden or strong cardboard box with perforations along the top and bottom of the sides. Place an electric lamp with a 60 watt bulb in the bottom and a mesh above this. The produce to be dried can be hung above the mesh or laid on racks before closing the box. The amount of time required to dry your produce will depend on many factors, so for the first few times it will be a case of trial and error: dry for a few hours, then test and decide whether longer is needed. Testing can be done by taste in the case of apple rings or similar, or by bending in the case of herbs or chillies – if they snap, that's dry enough; if they bend they need more drying.

Of course people have used the heat of the sun for drying food for thousands of years, and these days certain sun-dried products, such as tomatoes and raisins, are popular in many countries. But sun-drying often requires several days of hot sun and dry air – not something we can rely on in temperate countries. It is possible, however, to build a solar dryer which can work in cooler climates as described in the book: *The Solar Food Dryer: How to Make and Use Your Own Low-Cost, High-Performance, Sun-Powered Food Dehydrator* by Eben V. Fodor.

But when you can't rely on the weather, a great gadget for the produce-storer is an electric food dehydrator. There are several table-top units available which consist of a base unit containing the temperature and time controls, the heater and fan, and then a series of plastic drying trays which can be stacked on top. The food is usually sliced and laid out on the trays before the unit is set for the required amount of time and the correct temperature (which is detailed for each type of produce in the instructions which come with the unit). Dehydrators are clean, easy to use, and as they become increasingly popular are reducing in cost. These can be purchased over the internet or from specialist food shops.

VACUUM-PACKING

Keeping produce in a vacuum where the vast majority of air has been excluded can prolong the storage time considerably. There are two main reasons for this: firstly most of the airborne contaminants such as fungal spores or bacteria will have been extracted along with the air; and secondly the exclusion of air eliminates food degradation by oxidation, which is a reaction in the presence of oxygen which reduces food freshness, flavour and texture. Vacuum-packing has been used by the food-processing industry for many years, but is now starting to grow in popularity in the home as well. Some sources, for example, say that the same vegetable which would normally keep fresh in the fridge for seven days, would, if vacuum-packed, stay as fresh for twenty-five days.

The process can be as simple as using an inexpensive hand-operated vacuum pump to remove air from plastic bags after the produce has been bagged up, and this will be effective for food stored in the freezer, the fridge, and at ambient temperatures. But you can also now buy a domestic vacuum food sealer which is an electronic counter-top device, using special bags, which effectively pumps out the air and heat-seals the bag. These can be purchased over the internet or from specialist food shops.

Containers with special valves on the top can also be purchased for vacuum-packing. These are often made of polycarbonate in the shape of jars and pots and are very useful for storing produce such as nuts and dried fruits (as well as cooked produce such as biscuits and crisps). Air can be extracted from these with either a hand-operated or electric pump.

SALTING

For many centuries salting has been used as an important method for preserving food. In the past, salt was held in high value and has even given us the word 'salary', as Roman soldiers were paid wages in salt. It is best known for preserving meat and fish but can be used with some vegetables such as runner beans and cucumbers.

Sauerkraut, originating in eastern Europe, is basically salted cabbage that has been through a process of fermentation. Instructions for making this at home can be found in the Cabbages section in Part Two, page 58.

Note that table salt is not suitable due to the extra chemicals it contains; use sea salt or rock salt that has no additives. You will need roughly 1kg / 2½lb of salt per 3kg / 6½lb of vegetables. In general, salting vegetables entails layering them with salt in glass jar or earthenware pot, starting and ending with a layer of salt. A weight such as a saucer is placed on the top layer to keep the vegetables immersed in the brine which gradually forms. When the jar is full it can be topped with a tight-fitting lid and stored for up to a year.

Before using the vegetables – either cooked or in a salad – soak them in several changes of cold water for at least an hour to remove as much salt as possible.

BOTTLING

What can look better than rows of glass jars in the kitchen, full of brightly coloured and scrumptious-looking preserved fruits? Note that in some countries such as America, bottling is referred to as 'canning', although glass jars are still used; this is not to be confused with the commercial canning (these days in tin-coated steel cans) of food such as baked beans. Tin-canning is rarely seen in a home environment due to the equipment required, whereas glass-bottling can be done on a very small scale.

The idea is that the food in the bottles, or jars, is heated to a high-enough temperature, for a certain time, to kill the bacteria, yeasts and fungi, and to stop enzyme activity. As the jars are sealed at this high temperature there should be no reintroduction of spoiling micro-organisms. The acidity of the bottled produce is also an important factor in preventing contamination by the *botulinum* bacteria.

Although botulism (the disease caused by a neurotoxin produced when large numbers of the bacteria *Clostridium botulinum* die off) is rare, it can be lethal and can be associated with home-bottling, so it is vital to follow instructions carefully. The problem is that these particular bacteria can survive the normal boiling point of water (100°C/212°F), so if bottling low-acid foods, such as most vegetables, then you need to use a pressure canner (like a large pressure cooker specially made for bottling purposes). This allows you to reach a higher temperature that will kill the *botulinum* bacteria. In practice, most home-storers use other techniques for low-acid foods and reserve bottling for fruits that can be stored safely with this method. Discard bottled produce if you are in any doubt as to its safety. In particular do not use the contents if the lid comes off too easily as if it has lost its suction; if there are bubbles in the liquid; if the contents have changed colour or smell or taste unusual; or if there is any mould visible.

You need special strong bottling jars – either screw-topped or clip jars – both of which use rubber rings for sealing. You may know these as

Mason or Kilner jars, and they can be obtained from specialist shops or by mail order via the internet. Note that a perfect seal is essential and the rubber rings should only be used once. Fruit can be bottled in water or fruit juice, but a sugar syrup gives better colour and flavour (generally about 400g / 14oz of sugar per litre of water is used to make the syrup).

The bottles can either be heated in a large pan of water or in the oven. Whichever method you use, it is important to reach the right temperature for the right amount of time – these are detailed in Part Two.

Pan Method

Wash the jars, then sterilise by boiling in water for five minutes. Prepare your syrup by boiling the required amount of sugar in water. Prepare the fruit (this is detailed for each type of produce in Part Two), fill the sterilised jars with fruit, then top up with hot (60°C / 140° F) syrup. Tap the jars to dislodge air bubbles, or slide a knife carefully round the sides. Wet the rubber rings in boiling water and put the lids on the jars (fasten clips but do not tighten screw-tops), place the jars in the pan and completely cover with warm water. Note that the glass jars should not rest directly on the bottom of the pan but on a wire or wooden rack or even a pad of newspaper. Heat the water and simmer for the required amount of time. Then remove the jars, screw the lids tight, and leave to cool.

Oven Method

Heat the oven to 150°C / 300° F. Fill the jars with the fruit and boiling syrup as per the pan method, and then fit the lids (but not the metal screw bands – heat these separately in the oven). Place the jars on a pad of newspaper on a tray in the oven for the required amount of time, then remove and screw the hot bands on tightly – you'll need gloves for this! Leave the jars to cool.

In either case, after cooling, test for a good seal and vacuum by loosing the metal clip or band and lifting the bottle by the lid. If the lid stays firm, then refasten the fitting (if not, then freeze or refrigerate the jar and eat the contents as soon as possible). Screw-tops should be loosened very slightly for storage or they may be impossible to remove later.

Juices, purées and pulps can also be bottled using the above methods and, again, suggestions are mentioned throughout Part Two. Bottles of tomato purée (passata), for example, are very useful when making pasta sauces and many other dishes.

PICKLES AND CHUTNEYS

The difference between pickles and chutneys is that pickles are usually pieces of vegetable or fruit stored in vinegar, whereas chutneys are mixtures of chopped vegetables and fruits cooked in vinegar. So good old Branston Pickle is better described as chutney! In both cases it is the acid conditions produced by the vinegar which inhibit the actions of spoiling micro-organisms.

Most pickles and chutneys improve in flavour if left to mature for a few months, and will keep for several years. I suggest that you keep opened jars of chutney in the fridge, however.

A variety of vinegars can be used for pickling: malt, wine (sharp) or cider (fruity). Pickling vinegar is usually malt vinegar which has spices added, although sometimes distilled vinegar is used as it is clear and so improves the visibility of the pickled items. You can make your own pickling vinegar by steeping spices in the vinegar of your choice for a month or two before it is needed: add approximately 30g / 1½oz of mixed spices per litre of vinegar. Try a mixture of cinnamon, cloves, mace, allspice and peppercorns. Strain the spices out before the vinegar is used for pickling. Alternatively you can add mustard seeds and peppercorns (or even dried chilli peppers) to the jars of pickles. Similarly, vinegars can also be flavoured with sprigs of fresh herbs.

General pickling instructions

1. Choose young, unblemished vegetables; clean and cut to a suitable size while fresh.

2. Soak the vegetables in brine (100g / 3½oz) of salt dissolved in each litre of water), generally for 24 hours. This draws some water out of the vegetables, which improves their preservation. Alternatively they may be packed in salt for a day. Others, such as beetroot, may be cooked before pickling.

3. Pack the vegetables in jars and cover with vinegar by 1cm / ½ inch or more.

4. Put lids on tightly. As the acid vinegar will corrode metal, make sure that metal lids are either plastic-coated, or use wax paper under the lid.

Chutneys are for experimenters! All sorts of combinations of fruit and vegetables make great chutneys, and a number of guideline recipes are given in Part Two.

Basic chutney method

1. Finely chop all the fruit and vegetables (or use a mincer or food processor). Onions and spices nearly always feature in chutneys, other common additions are apples, raisins and tomatoes.

2. Place in a large pan (NOT iron or copper, which would react with the acidic vinegar) with salt, sugar, vinegar and spices of your choice (quantities are suggested in recipes throughout Part Two, but in general, for each 4kg / 9lb of fruit/vegetable, add about 20g / ¾oz salt, 400g / 14oz sugar and 500ml to 1 litre / 1 – 2 pints of vinegar).

3. Simmer until tender – 30 minutes to 3 hours depending on ingredients.

4. Sterilise jars by boiling in water in a large pan for five to ten minutes, or placing in an oven at 160°C / 320°F for at least ten minutes. Spoon the chutney into the sterile jars while hot, put lids on tightly and store in a cool, dark place.

RELISHES, KETCHUPS AND SAUCES

First some definitions: in general, **relishes** are very similar to chutneys except they are usually more finely textured and may resemble a chunky sauce. **Ketchups** and **sauces** are often sieved to give a creamy, lump-free consistency, the difference between the two being that ketchups have one predominant flavour (e.g. tomato or mushroom ketchup) whereas sauces have a larger number of ingredients.

They all involve a certain amount of vinegar in their preparation, and so iron and copper utensils should be avoided; the same equipment you use for chutney-making will be perfect. All should be stored in sterilised jars or bottles with airtight lids; some require a period in a water bath similar to the bottling process – timings and details are given in individual recipes throughout Part Two. The finished products will store for several months, and once opened should be kept in a fridge.

JAMS AND JELLIES

Jams

Home-made jam – you can't beat it. It's not only a good way of storing surplus fruit for the winter, it's a great way of eating it too!

The preservation works by a combination of the boiling stage (which kills micro-organisms and de-activates enzymes) and the high sugar content of the product (which inhibits the growth of bacteria that may contaminate the jam later). Low sugar jam can be made, but it will be more runny, will need to be kept in the fridge and will not store as long.

There are whole books dedicated to jam-making, so I'm not going into too much detail here, but let's look at the basics:

Basic jam method

1. Choose fruit that is just ripe or nearly ripe for jam-making. Over-ripe fruit has little pectin and will make a runny jam.

2. Pectin (a gum-like substance in cell walls) and acid are both important in getting jam to set. Fruits high in both are apples, currants, gooseberries and plums. If your strawberry jam is just too runny, then either combine the fruit with one rich in pectin and acid, or add commercial pectins and lemon juice. Another alternative is to buy jam-makers' sugar which has added pectin and acid; the packet will display instructions for its use. Individual jam recipes in Part Two suggest where extra pectin or acid may be needed. **Pectin test:** if you

are not sure of the pectin content of your fruit, then perform the following test: put one teaspoon of juice from the simmered fruit into a glass and, when cool, add one tablespoon of methylated spirits and swirl together. If a lump of clear jelly forms, the fruit has a good level of pectin, but if the jelly is soft and breaks into smaller pieces there is a low pectin content and you will need to add more for the jam to set properly.

3. Heat the washed and chopped fruit in a large pan, adding a little water if necessary to prevent burning. Do not use iron pans, which will react with the acidic fruit and taint the flavour. Simmer for 15 -45 minutes until the fruit has broken down to a pulp. Soft fruits like strawberries and raspberries will not need any extra water added and will only require 15 minutes simmering.

4. Add the sugar: 60% by weight. This percentage is crucial: too low and the jam may ferment, too high and the sugar will crystallise during storage. Stir with a long-handled wooden spoon to dissolve the sugar, bring back to the boil, then stir as little as possible.

5. Boil hard until setting point – this may be a few minutes or even up to twenty, depending on the type and quantity of fruit and how well it was cooked before the sugar was added. To test for setting point: place a small blob of the mixture on a cold plate; after one minute it should have formed a skin which wrinkles when you touch it. Take the pan off the heat while waiting for this test result or you may overshoot and end up with very hard jam. An alternative is the flake test: scoop a little jam onto the wooden spoon and allow it to cool for a few seconds. Then turn the spoon on its side: if the jam dribbles off quickly it has not boiled enough, but if it runs together and drops off slowly in large flakes then it has reached setting point. If you make a lot of jam, you may like to get a special sugar thermometer; most jams will have reached setting point when the thermometer reads 105°C / 220°F.

6. Remove from the heat immediately, skim off any scum from the surface with a slotted spoon, then stir and ladle the jam into sterilised jars which have been warmed in the oven (or boiled in water for five to ten minutes). You may find a jug and funnel easier to use when filling jars, especially if you are making large quantities. You can buy new jars for jam from specialist shops or via the internet, or

better still, recycle bought jam jars and ask your neighbours to save them for you.

7. Cover the surface of the jam with a waxed disc (wax side down) and then top the jar with either a cellulose cover held with an elastic band, or a plastic-coated metal lid screwed on tight while hot. Boil metal lids first to ensure they are sterile. You can obtain waxed discs and covers at your local store, in supermarkets or via the internet.

8. Cool, label (type of jam and date), store, eat, enjoy!

Note that the addition of 60% by weight of sugar is critical for the best preservation, as any less than this will allow micro-organisms to start the jam fermenting in storage. So don't forget to weigh your fruit before you start heating it and calculate the amount of sugar that will be required. After opening it is a good idea to keep jars of jam in the fridge – especially if the proportion of sugar is suspect – to reduce growth of yeasts, bacteria or fungi.

Jellies

Jellies are essentially jams made out of the fruit's juice; they should be clear, brightly-coloured and packed with flavour. The same rules regarding pectin and acid apply. You will need something to strain the fruit pulp: either a purpose-made jelly-bag, often made out of nylon, or a large piece of muslin. You will also need a means of supporting the bag over the collecting bowl: if you do not have a jelly bag stand you can improvise by tying the bag to the legs of an upturned stool or chair so that it hangs over the bowl which has been placed on the upside down seat. Always boil your muslin bag (or whatever material you use for straining) before and after use.

Basic jelly method

1. After cooking the fruit to a pulp (usually 45-60 minutes of simmering), ladle it into your straining bag and leave until the juice has stopped dripping through. Note that this can take anything from one to ten hours. Slow straining is essential for a clear jelly to result – do not be tempted to push or squeeze it through.

2. Pour the juice into a pan, bring to the boil and add the sugar. The amount of sugar will depend partly on the pectin content of the fruit: if high in pectin allow 1kg / 2½lb of sugar per litre of juice; if

only moderate levels of pectin, reduce to 600g / 1lb 5oz of sugar per litre of juice. Stir with a long-handled wooden spoon to dissolve, and bring back to the boil, then stir as little as possible.

3. Boil hard for ten minutes and then test for setting point in the same way you would for jam.

4. When setting point has been reached, remove the pan from the heat immediately, skim off any scum from the surface with a slotted spoon, then stir and ladle the jelly into sterilised jars which have been warmed in the oven.

5. Cover the surface of the jelly in exactly the same way as you would jam. Cool, label (type of jelly and date), store, eat, enjoy!

A number of recipes for jams and jellies are suggested in Part Two, but again, experimentation with mixtures of fruits can yield satisfying results. Note that a 'conserve' is usually the term given to a jam that has other ingredients added: apricot and almond conserve for example is simply apricot jam that has had chopped almonds mixed in after the jam has set.

FRUIT BUTTERS AND CHEESES

A fruit butter is essentially made by cooking a fruit until it becomes a paste. This can be spread on toast as an alternative to butter and jam, eaten with pancakes or as an ice-cream topping amongst other things. There are also the advantages that fruit butters have a lower sugar content than jam, and thicken without the need for pectin.

Fruit cheeses are less commonly made but are basically butters that have been cooked further until they are of a more solid consistency and can be sliced; they may be eaten with bread as you would a normal cheese – excellent for those on a dairy-free diet.

Fruit butters and cheeses can be frozen, but it is more common to jar them up, as you would jam. They will then keep for a few months, but should be refrigerated after opening. Many improve in flavour if left for a few weeks before eating. A variety of fruits and combinations can be made into butters, those most often used being: apples, apricots, blackcurrants, grapes, peaches, pears and plums. Spices can also be added as desired: cinnamon, ginger or allspice for example. Some fruits, such as apples and pears, will need a little water, juice or cider added whilst cooking. There are various suggestions throughout Part Two but the basic method for preparation is as follows:

Basic method for fruit butters and cheeses

1. Cut the fruit into small pieces, and place in a thick-bottomed pan with up to half as much liquid if required. Bring to the boil, then simmer until the fruit is soft. Push through a sieve and then purée in a food processor or with a hand-held blender.

2. Put the pulp back in the pan and cook slowly, stirring all the time, until the mixture is thick. Add half as much sugar (e.g. 250g / 8oz sugar for 500g / 1lb fruit) and any spices you want, then boil until thick and creamy and no free liquid is left in the pan.

3. Pour into sterilised jars and top with lids or waxed discs and cellulose covers as you would for jam.

If you are making fruit cheese, then add a larger amount of sugar – up to the same amount as fruit pulp – and boil the mixture for longer until it is stiff. The cheese can be stored in the same way as fruit butter, but use a wide-topped jar or pot so that it can be removed easily on to a plate when needed.

FERMENTING

It is the alcohol produced during fermentation that inhibits the growth of micro-organisms which could spoil the product. This enables us to store brewed drinks for many years (although they inevitably deteriorate in quality after a certain time).

As there are many detailed books on the home-brewing of ciders, wines and beers, this is not the place to compete with them. The making of cider is explored more in Part Two under Apples (page 34), but as so many fruits and vegetables can be made into wines we'll discuss some of the basics here.

The general idea is that yeasts (usually introduced, although natural ones do occur on the surface of most fruits) grow and multiply using sugar, and produce alcohol as a result. Cleanliness is vital at all stages to prevent fungi and other micro-organisms from spoiling the end product. All equipment and bottles must be sterilised before use, either by boiling or by washing with a chemical sterilising solution.

Basic fermenting method

1. Wash the fruits or vegetables, then chop, crush, mash or press.

2. Add boiling water (sometimes simmering is needed) and leave this mixture for a day.

3. Strain the mixture then add sugar and yeast before pouring into demijohns or other vessels. Fit these with fermentation locks (to exclude air, which will contain undesirable micro-organisms, but allowing gases to escape). If juice such as grape juice is being used to make the wine, it can go straight into the demijohn with the yeast, omitting stage 2.

4. Leave the demijohns in a warm place for the mixture to ferment – this could take a month or two.

5. 'Racking' is the procedure of siphoning the liquid into a clean vessel while leaving the sediment behind. This may be required a couple of times during the fermentation until the wine is clear.

6. When fermentation has ceased, rack the liquid into sterile bottles before corking and storing somewhere cool and dark. Most wines improve after a few months – some need a year or more.

Almost any fruit or vegetable can be made into wine. For specific techniques and recipes you should consult a wine-making book, although many suggestions are scattered throughout Part Two.

Part Two

The Produce

APPLES

There are thousands of varieties of this popular and hardy fruit available, offering a wide range of flavours, textures and uses. Dwarfing rootstocks now mean that even the smallest garden can contain a number of apple trees, and a wise choice of cultivars will mean you can have apples ripening from mid-summer to late winter.

Windfalls and early maturing varieties do not store so well, so use these to make jam and chutney. Cooking apples are the best for jam-making because of their high acid content. Try dried apple rings as a great snack or a useful addition to lunch boxes. Late maturing apple varieties will be sweeter – so are the best for juice and making cider.

Recommended varieties
There are a huge number of varieties available – here are a few suggestions:

Eating apples
Cox's Orange Pippin (a superb dessert apple that keeps particularly well)
Worcester Pearmain (bright red fruits with a sweet flavour)
Egremont Russet (crisp, sweet fruits with a nutty flavour)
Sunset (heavy cropper of small but delicious fruits)
Red Falstaff (green/red fruits with a crisp and juicy flavour)

Cooking apples
Bramley (large fruits which keep particularly well)
Lord Derby (heavy crop of bright green fruits with a sweet flavour)

Crab apple
John Downie (large conical yellow crab apples flushed red which are considered to be the best for jelly and wine making)

Dry storage
For later-ripening fruit. Use only perfect specimens. Wrap them individually in paper and place gently in crates or on shelves in a cool, frost-free, but not too dry place. They should keep until spring.

Jam

Apples are often added to other fruits which may be lacking in acid for jam-making – for example see Blackberry and Apple Jam under Blackberries (page 51). Crab apples are particularly high in pectin and acid so small amounts are very useful as additions to other jams.

Freeze

Apples can be frozen either fresh after peeling and removing the core, or after stewing and cooling for later use in pies, crumbles etc.

Chutney

Apples are a useful addition to a variety of chutneys – for example see Marrow and Apple Chutney under Squashes (page 127) and Green Tomato Chutney under Tomatoes (page 135).

Apple juice

Extract the juice using a fruit press or electric juicer. Freshly-pressed juice will keep only for a day or two in the fridge before fermenting, but don't forget to freeze some. This can be done in plastic bags inside small boxes (e.g. juice cartons) – when frozen the boxes can be removed and the blocks of juice packed together. Empty plastic milk cartons can also be used for freezing juice but they must be thoroughly cleaned, and don't forget to leave a 5cm / 2 inch space for expansion as the juice freezes.

Cider

It's best to use a mixture of apple varieties when making cider – a good way to use up over-ripe and bruised apples that wouldn't store well by other means. As with wine-making it is important that all the equipment used is clean.

You can start drinking it at Christmas (assuming you started fermentation in October) although it will continue to improve if you can bear to leave some of it any longer!

DRIED APPLE RINGS

Core the fruit and cut into rings about 5mm thick.

Place for a few minutes in a mixture of 300ml / 10 fl oz water plus 150ml / 5 fl oz lemon juice and a teaspoon of sugar (this stops the rings discolouring).

Drain the rings before drying them on a rack in an oven, drying box or food dehydrator. This can take up to one day depending on the method.

Once the fruit feels dry and squeezing produces no juice, it can be jarred up and sealed.

The product can be eaten dry as a snack or soaked for a day in water before adding to recipes.

APPLE AND SLOE JELLY

1.5kg / 3½ lb apples
2kg / 4½ lb sloes
1.5 litres water / 3 pints
Sugar

Place washed sloes in a pan, cover with water, bring to the boil, then simmer until it forms a pulp.

Do the same to the chopped and peeled apples in a separate pan. Strain both pulps and then combine in a further pan.

Test for pectin (see Part One, pages 27-30) and add if necessary.

Bring the combined juice to the boil, then for every litre / 2 pints of liquid add 750g / 10lb 2 oz of sugar. Stir to dissolve the sugar, bring to the boil and boil hard until setting point. Jar up and seal.

APPLE BUTTER

2kg / 4½ lb apples (a mix of crab apples and cultivated varieties produces a fine butter)
1 litre / 2 pints of water
1 litre / 2 pints of cider
Sugar
2 teaspoons of ground cloves and cinnamon

Cut the peeled fruit into small pieces and place in a thick-bottomed pan with the water and cider.

Bring to the boil, then simmer until the fruit is soft.

Push through a sieve and then put the pulp back in the pan and cook slowly, stirring all the time, until the mixture thickens up.

Add 750g / 1lb 10oz sugar per 1kg / 2½ lb of fruit, and the spices, then boil until thick.

Pour into sterilised jars and top with lids or waxed discs and cellulose as you would for jam.

APPLE SAUCE

1kg / 2½ lb apples
1 tablespoon sugar
250ml / ½ pint water
25g / 1oz butter
5 cloves
1 teaspoon ginger

Wash and chop the apples, then simmer in a pan with the other ingredients until soft. Sieve the mixture and pour into warm glass bottles or jars.

Top with an airtight lid and heat in a water bath at 77°C / 170°F for 30 minutes. Tighten lid and store.

The sauce will store for several months and should be kept in a fridge once opened.

MAKING CIDER

Wash the apples and chop them roughly. Then crush them by pounding with a heavy wooden post in a strong bucket, or use a purpose-built crusher (there is a simple and effective one available which consists of a plastic bucket with a spinning/slicing device that attaches to a standard power drill). Put the pulp in a fruit press and apply pressure to extract the juice. Pour the juice into a demijohn (or suitable fermenting vessel) and add brewer's yeast. Fit a fermentation lock (to exclude air, which will contain undesirable micro-organisms) and leave in a warm place to ferment – this could take a couple of weeks. Rack the liquid (siphon into a clean vessel while leaving the sediment behind) once or twice during the fermentation until the cider is clear. When fermentation has ceased, rack the cider into sterile bottles and store somewhere cool and dark.

■ ■ ■

ARTICHOKES (GLOBE)

Globe artichokes (derived from cardoons) are perennial plants that produce large green thistle-like heads with edible pads at the base of the outer scales. The heads should be harvested before they flower in the summer, and then they will be followed by a further crop of smaller ones. They will keep for a week in the fridge if the flower stalks are stood in water which is refreshed daily.

Recommended varieties

Green Globe (traditional green heads)
Purple Globe Romanesco (very attractive purple heads)

Freeze

Remove the outer leaves and stalks of small heads and blanch for 6 minutes before cooling and freezing in plastic bags. To cook from frozen, boil for about 10 minutes.

GLOBE ARTICHOKE PICKLE

Cover the small heads, or removed scales of larger artichokes, in layers of salt and leave overnight. Rinse thoroughly in fresh water the next day, dry and pack into jars, covering with the vinegar of your choice before sealing.

GLOBE ARTICHOKE SOUP

If you have an abundance of globes you can make larger quantities of this soup and freeze it in batches.

4 large artichokes
Juice of 2 lemons
1 onion
75g / 2½ oz butter

1 litre / 2 pints of milk
Double cream
Salt and pepper

Cut off about two thirds of the top of each artichoke scale and discard.

Now cut away each scale from the soft base of the globe and place them in a bowl of water with juice of a lemon added to prevent discolouration. Do not use the layer of papery leaves or hairs.

Simmer the scales in a pan of water with juice from the other lemon for 20 minutes. Drain and cool.

Melt the butter in a large saucepan, and cook the sliced onion for 5 minutes. Stir in the artichoke scales and cook for a further 5 minutes.

Add the milk and bring to the boil, then simmer for 10 minutes.

Process the mixture with a food blender. You can sieve the soup, if you want a smoother texture.

Add salt and pepper to taste and a spoonful of cream to each bowl.

■ ■ ■

ARTICHOKES (JERUSALEM)

The knobbly tubers of Jerusalem artichokes have a distinctive taste and are an interesting alternative to potatoes. They can be cooked in all the same ways: roasted, baked, fried, boiled and so on, and can even be eaten raw. Jerusalem artichokes can be harvested from autumn onwards and left in the ground until they are needed. If you are expecting very hard frosts then either cover the plants with a thick layer of straw, or heel them into dry ground near the house. Once harvested, the tubers will keep fresh for a few weeks if kept in a plastic bag in the fridge.

Save a few tubers to replant for a crop the following year, or simply leave some in the ground (the latter is often done inadvertently and the crop can be notoriously invasive).

Recommended variety

Fuseau (produces smoother than usual tubers that are easy to peel)

Dry storage

Pack the tubers in sand in boxes. In a cool, frost-free building they should keep for a few months.

Freeze

The tubers of Jerusalem artichokes can be cooked and mashed to a purée before cooling and freezing in plastic boxes or bags. This purée can be used later in soups.

JERUSALEM ARTICHOKE WINE

An interesting wine can be made from Jerusalem artichokes. See Part One (pages 31-32) for general instructions.
Scrub and slice 3kg / 6½ lb of tubers
Boil with 1kg / 2½ lb sugar in 5 litres / 10 pints of water.
Cool, add the yeast, and ferment in suitable vessels.
When fermentation has ceased, rack the liquid into sterile bottles, cork and store somewhere cool and dark.

■ ■ ■

ASPARAGUS

Asparagus plants are perennial and may produce edible young shoots, known as spears, for up to twenty years or so. The spears will appear in May and should be cut when they have reached about 15cm / 6 inches tall. Cut them 5cm / 2 inches below the soil surface with a long knife. Established plants can be cut over an eight week period. Note that male and female plants are available, the male ones being more highly productive in terms of spears.

The quality of asparagus declines rapidly after cutting. It will only keep for a few days in the fridge, but standing the spears upright in a mug of water will extend this a little (change the water daily). For longer storage, freezing is the best option.

Recommended varieties

Connover's Colossal (a favourite variety producing good-sized spears)
Amarus (fine spears with a sharper taste)
Crimson Pacific (produces purple spears)

Freeze

Immediately after cutting, wash well, then blanch for 2 minutes (or 4 minutes for thick stems). Cool then pack in plastic containers and freeze. To cook from frozen, boil for about 4 minutes.

ASPARAGUS SOUP

If you have an abundance of spears you can make larger quantities of this soup and freeze it in batches. It is also a good way of using spears that are a little woody or beyond their best.

500g / 1lb asparagus spears
1 onion
20g / ¾oz butter
2 teaspoons olive oil
150ml / 5fl oz double cream
1 garlic clove
750ml / 1½ pints vegetable stock
Mixed herbs
Lemon juice
Salt and pepper

Melt the butter in a large pan with the oil.
Add the chopped onion and crushed garlic and fry gently for 5 minutes.
Chop the washed asparagus spears, add to the pan and fry for a further 5 minutes.
Add the stock and herbs, cover and simmer for 10 minutes.
Process the mixture with a food blender.
Add the juice of a lemon and salt and pepper to taste.
Finally add the cream and reheat before serving.

■ ■ ▓

AUBERGINES

It is quite easy to grow aubergines (also known as eggplants because of the ovoid shape of the fruits) in a greenhouse or polytunnel, and they are becoming increasingly popular. Although best known for shiny purple fruits, aubergines actually come in a variety of colours and shapes. Do not let the fruits grow too large, but cut when about 15cm / 6 inches long and before the skin loses its shine (July to October, depending on the variety). Remove any fruits that start to form from late summer onwards – this will encourage the remaining ones to grow and ripen. The fruits stay usable for several weeks in the fridge or can be frozen straight away or made into chutney or brinjal pickle.

Recommended varieties

Long Purple (deep violet fruits)
Très Hâtive de Barbentane (prolific variety that matures well in cooler climates)
Rosa Bianca (round pinky-white fruits with a mild creamy flavour)
Little Finger (produces clusters of small fruits)
Black Beauty (dark glossy oval fruits that mature early)

Freeze

After peeling, cut the aubergine into thick slices or chunks and then blanch for 4 minutes. Cool and open-freeze before packing into containers, otherwise the fruit will form a solid mass that cannot be separated later in its frozen state. Thaw before adding to dishes (such as moussaka and ratatouille) for cooking, or cook from frozen for 5 minutes.

Alternatively, aubergine slices can be frozen in a cooked state: slice the fruits, sprinkle with salt and leave for half an hour to remove excess water, then pat dry with kitchen paper before frying in oil. Cool and open-freeze the slices before packing into containers, as before.

AUBERGINE CHUTNEY

1 kg / 2½ lb aubergines
350g / 12 oz onions
500g / 1 lb apples
650g / 1 lb 6oz sugar
20g / ¾oz salt
300ml / 10 fl oz white wine vinegar
50g / 2 oz ginger and pickling spices

Slice and chop the aubergines, onions and apples and place in a pan with all the other ingredients except the sugar.
Bring to the boil and simmer until tender before stirring in the sugar and boiling the mixture until it is thick.
Jar up and seal.
This chutney is best if left for a month before eating. Refrigerate jars after opening.
A successful alternative can be made using a mixture of aubergines and capsicum peppers.

BRINJAL PICKLE

This is a traditional accompaniment to Indian food and there are many variations on the basic recipe below. Unlike aubergine chutney, this pickle should be eaten straight away and will only last a couple of weeks in the fridge, so it is usually made in smaller quantities. Out of season it can be made from aubergines that you have previously frozen.

1 large aubergine
1 onion
10 garlic cloves
2-3 cm / 1 inch piece of root ginger
2 chillies
1 teaspoon chilli powder
1 teaspoon garam masala
100ml / 3 fl oz white wine vinegar
200ml / 7 fl oz olive oil

Finely chop and fry the onions gently in the oil for 5 minutes on a low heat.
Cut the aubergine into very small pieces and add to the pan with the chopped chillies and ginger, crushed garlic and all other ingredients. Simmer for 30 minutes. Jar up and seal.

■ ■ ■

BEANS – BROAD

Broad beans, also known as fava beans, are cool-season annual plants that produce a highly nutritious seed packed with protein. They are generally sown in autumn for spring/summer harvesting, but can also be sown in early spring. The young pods can be harvested whole, or the immature seeds removed from larger pods. Freezing is a good option for storing broad beans, but some varieties freeze better than others – check the details on seed packets. Large tough beans do not become tender by freezing, so harvest when small and tender. They can also be dried or made into wine.

Recommended varieties

Express (fast to mature if sown early spring, freeze well)
Red Epicure (an early variety with red beans)
Green Windsor (large beans, sow in spring, freeze well)
Aquadulce Claudia (sow in November for an early crop the next year)

Freeze

After washing the shelled beans, blanch for 1 or 2 minutes depending on size. Cool and open-freeze then bag up. To cook from frozen, boil for about 6 minutes.

Dry

Leave the pods on the plants until they have turned yellow, then cut the plant at ground level and hang indoors to dry completely. When the pods have become brittle, shell the beans and leave on trays for a few days. Then store in a cool dry place in airtight containers. Soak the beans before cooking.

BROAD BEAN WINE

See Part One (pages 31-32) for general instructions.

Boil 2kg / 4½ lb of shelled beans in 5 litres / 10 pints of water. Do not split or mash the beans but strain off the liquid.

Add sugar and yeast to the cooled liquid, and ferment.

When fermentation has ceased, rack the liquid into sterile bottles, cork and store somewhere cool and dark.

■ ■ ■

BEANS – FRENCH

Pick the pods of French beans while young and tender and eat or freeze as soon as possible after harvesting. If the pods are young there will be no need to string them. A few plants sown early in the greenhouse will provide beans from June onwards, those planted outside will crop later in the summer and autumn. Let a number of plants grow on unharvested to provide beans for drying later in the year. There are a large number of varieties suitable for drying – many of which produce attractively coloured beans – see below for recommendations. Don't forget to save some of your beans for sowing next spring.

Recommended varieties

Slenderette (maincrop, pods freeze well)
Purple Queen (produces distinctive purple pods)
Tendergreen (pods freeze well)
Canadian Wonder (use the young pods whole or leave to mature, harvest the red beans and use in casseroles and chilli dishes)

The following varieties are recommended for drying:
Brown Dutch (golden brown beans)
Marie Louise (pink/purple two-tone beans)
Czar (large white butter beans)

Pea Bean (interestingly coloured white/brown beans that some say resemble tiny killer whales!)
Borlotto Lingua di Fuoco (purple and white beans in beautiful red pods)
Cannellino (white beans, good for home-made baked beans – see recipe below)

Freeze

Wash, trim the ends off and string if necessary. Blanch for 2 minutes before cooling and packing in plastic bags. To cook from frozen, boil for about 5 minutes.

Dry

Note that some varieties are more suited to this than others. Leave the pods on the plants until they have turned yellow, then cut the plant at ground level and hang indoors to dry completely. When the pods have become brittle, shell the beans and leave on trays for a few days. Then store in a cool dry place in airtight containers. They will keep for months and can be added to stews or made into casseroles or home-made baked beans. Soak the beans overnight before cooking. Drain, rinse, boil vigorously for ten minutes then simmer until tender.

BAKED BEANS

There are numerous varied recipes for home-made baked beans – this is one of my favourites:

400g / 14oz dried beans (e.g. Cannellino)
1 large onion
1 garlic clove
2 tablespoons olive oil
1 tablespoon paprika
2 tablespoons tomato paste
1 red pepper
450g / 1lb can of tomatoes (or fresh and skinned)
150ml / 5fl oz water, salt and pepper, soured cream

Soak the beans in cold water overnight.
Drain and simmer in a pan of fresh water for 45 minutes then drain again.
Heat the oil in a pan and add the sliced onion and crushed garlic, fry for 5 minutes then add the paprika and fry for a further 5 minutes.

Add the beans, tomato paste, finely chopped red pepper, chopped tomatoes and water. Bring to the boil and simmer for fifteen minutes.

Add salt and pepper to taste and stir in 4 tablespoons of the soured cream before serving.

■ ■ ■

BEANS – RUNNER

These climbers are actually perennials but are grown as annuals in cool climates. Harvest the flat pods of runner beans while young and tender, leaving some on the plants to mature, for collecting the beans for drying and sowing again next year. Pick the pods from July to September – picking regularly maintains cropping. Freezing is a good option for runner beans, but some varieties freeze better than others – check the details on seed packets. They can also be dried or salted.

Recommended varieties

Red Flame (early maturing)
Enorma Elite (crops over a long period)
Desirée (pods freeze well)
Sun Bright (late maturing – harvest August to October)

Freeze

Wash, trim the ends off and string the beans. Slice into short lengths and blanch for 2 minutes before cooling and packing in plastic bags. To cook from frozen, boil for about 5 minutes.

Dry

These can be dried in the same way as French beans. Leave the pods on the plants until they have turned yellow, then cut the plant at ground level and hang indoors to dry completely. When the pods have become brittle, shell the beans and leave on trays for a few days. Then store in a cool dry place in airtight containers. Soak the beans before cooking.

SALTED BEANS

This is an old method for storing beans which is still favoured by some today. Use 1kg / 2½lb kitchen salt for every 3kg / 6½lb beans. Wash, string and slice the beans, pack in glass jars with layers of salt and beans, press down and cover. After a few days the beans will have shrunk down as the water is drawn out – add more beans and salt to fill the jar again. A thick brine is formed in the jar which will preserve the beans for a year or more. When needed, wash the beans well, soak in warm water for an hour, rinse and simmer in unsalted water until tender.

■ ■ ■

BEETROOT

In the 17th century beetroot was boiled and eaten, as in its native Italy, with oil and vinegar, or often with vinegar alone. It made a boiled salad on its own and supplied a richly coloured garnish for other salads. Vinegar was loved by the English (an Italian called Castelvetro who lived in England in Elizabethan times complained that English salads were swimming in vinegar) and pickled beetroot was enjoyed for the taste as well as being a storage method.

Pull beetroots for storage before they get too large and woody: from July to October. Twist the foliage off (cutting causes bleeding of the beets).

Recommended varieties

Early Wonder (can be sown in March or even February with protection – produces large roots and is resistant to bolting)

Egyptian Turnip Rooted (quick growing with a great flavour, excellent for eating raw, large roots with a deep red colour)

Detroit Globe (favoured by exhibitors due to the large roots and smooth skins – a bright maroon colour)

Barabietola di Chioggia (this is an old traditional Italian beetroot, good for eating raw or cooked, roots are rosy-pink coloured with the flesh having attractive concentric rings of white and pink)

Freeze

Small beetroots should first be washed and boiled whole for 1 or 2 hours in salted water. Then the skins can be rubbed off (if desired), before slicing and packing in containers when cool.

Dry storage

Gently remove the soil from undamaged beets and pack in sand in boxes. In a cool, frost-free building they should keep until spring.

PICKLED BEETROOT

Boil and skin as above before covering with vinegar in suitable jars.
Either slice or, if small, pickle whole.
Pickled beetroot can be used after a week and will be at its best for 3 months.

BEETROOT WINE

See Part One (pages 31-32) for general instructions.
Boil 2kg / 4½lb of diced, unpeeled beetroot in 3 litres / 6 pints water for 30 minutes.
Strain, stir in 1.75kg / 4lb sugar, and add the juice of a lemon.
Add yeast to the cooled liquid, and ferment.
When fermentation has ceased, rack the liquid into sterile bottles, cork and store somewhere cool and dark.
If you like ginger you may like to try adding some crushed ginger root with the lemon juice.

BORSCHT

The original base for this bright red Polish and Russian soup was the cow parsnip – in fact the Russian word 'borscht' means cow parsnip. Today, borscht is a beetroot soup, usually made with beetroot, stock, cabbage, and frequently potatoes and other root vegetables. There is a large variety of recipes for this soup – try this simple one for a winter-warmer:

4 large beetroots with tops
1 medium onion sliced
1 teaspoon salt
2 cloves garlic
Juice of 1 lemon
3 litres water / 5 pints
500g / 1lb unpeeled potatoes cut into small chunks
1 tablespoon cider or wine vinegar
Brown sugar to taste

Cut off the beetroot tops, wash, chop, and set aside.
Peel the beetroots, shred or grate and put them into a large pan.
Add the onion, salt, crushed garlic, lemon, and water to the pan, cover and bring to the boil.
Simmer gently for about 20 minutes.
Add the potatoes, vinegar and chopped beetroot tops.
Simmer for a further 10 minutes until the potatoes are soft.
Season to taste, creating a sweet and sour flavour, with salt, sugar, and lemon juice. Serve hot with crusty bread.
If you like, you can cook this soup in larger batches and freeze it in portions.

■ ■ ■

BLACKBERRIES

Pick blackberries when sun-ripened for the best flavour. They are low in acid so are often mixed with other fruit, such as apples, when making jam. Although there are some super varieties available for cultivation – some with no thorns and a great flavour, don't forget nature provides an abundant supply for free down many country lanes.

Recommended varieties

Bedford Giant (an early variety with rampant growth)
Karaka Black (large juicy berries, long fruiting season)
Chester (high-yielding on upright, spine-free canes)
Waldo (large highly flavoured fruits on thornless canes)

Freeze

Fresh after removing stalks (open-freeze then bag up). They can also be frozen as a purée after stewing, sieving and cooling.

Bottle

See Part One (pages 23-24) for methods. If heating in water, heat to simmering (88°C / 190°F) in 30 minutes and hold this for a further 2 minutes. If heating in the oven, keep at 150°C / 300°F for 40 minutes (for up to 2kg / 4½lb fruit) or for 60 minutes (for up to 5kg / 11lb fruit). Blackberries can also be bottled mixed with apples in layers.

BLACKBERRY AND APPLE JAM

2kg / 4½lb blackberries
1kg / 2½lb cooking apples
400ml / 13 fl oz water
3kg / 6½lb sugar

Simmer the peeled and sliced apples and the blackberries until soft in separate pans with half the water each.
Then mix together with the sugar, stir, boil, and keep boiling hard to setting point.
Jar up and seal.
If you prefer a seedless jam you can sieve the blackberry pulp before adding to the apple mixture.

BLACKBERRY JELLY

2kg / 4½lb blackberries
500ml / 1 pint water
Sugar

Simmer the washed fruit in the water until tender.
Mash the berries and strain before doing a pectin test (see pages 27-30 for details) and adding sugar (if high in pectin allow 1kg / 2½ lb of sugar per litre of juice; if only moderate levels of pectin, reduce to 600g / 1lb 5 oz of sugar per litre of juice).
Bring back to the boil, then boil hard for ten minutes before testing for setting point. When this has been reached, remove the pan from the heat, skim off any scum from the surface, then ladle the jelly into sterilised jars.
Cover and store.

BLACKBERRY CHUTNEY

3kg / 6½ lb blackberries
1kg / 2lb 3 oz apples
1kg / 2lb 3 oz onions
25g / 1 oz salt
1kg / 2lb 3 oz sugar
1 litre / 2 pints vinegar
Spices of your choice (e.g. ginger, pepper, mustard)

Finely chop the apples and onions and add to the blackberries in a large pan. Add the vinegar, salt and spices and simmer for 1 hour.
Sieve the chutney to remove the pips, then add the sugar.
Stir and simmer until it reaches a pulpy consistency. Jar up and seal.

BLACKBERRY CHEESE

2kg / 4½ lb blackberries
1kg / 2lb 3oz cooking apples
600ml / 1.2 pints water
Sugar

Peel and cut the apples into small pieces and place in a thick-bottomed pan with the blackberries and water.
Bring to the boil, then simmer until the fruit is soft.
Push through a sieve and then put the pulp back in the pan and cook slowly, stirring all the time, until the mixture is thick.
Add the same weight in sugar then boil until it has reached the required consistency. Spoon into sterilised pots and top with lids or waxed discs and cellulose as you would for jam.

BLACKBERRY WINE

See Part One (pages 31-32) for general instructions.
Dissolve 2kg / 4½ lb sugar in 5 litres / 10 pints of boiling water.
When cool, add this liquid to 2kg / 4½ lb of mashed blackberries.
Add the yeast, the juice of 2 lemons and ferment.
When fermentation has ceased, rack the liquid into sterile bottles, cork and store somewhere cool and dark.

■ ■ ■

BLACK CURRANTS, RED AND WHITE CURRANTS, JOSTABERRIES AND CHOKEBERRIES

Pick when ripe and juicy! They may be fiddly to harvest and fiddly to prepare (after removing the stalk and calyx [top brown bit] from each currant you will have purple hands for sure) but it is well worth it. Black currant jam is a favourite and the freshly pressed juice tastes unbelievable – and is very good for you! Red currants can be made into an excellent jelly, or bottle mixed with raspberries.

Jostaberries are a black currant x gooseberry hybrid, producing delicious sharp-flavoured fruits twice the size of black currants, which can be used to make jams, pies and summer puddings.

Chokeberries are bushy shrubs which produce fruits that look like large black currants. Both jostaberries and chokeberries can be used in all the same recipes and ways as black currants.

Recommended varieties

Ben Connan (high-yielding black currant with large berries)
Ben Alder (excellent black currant variety for juicing)
Jonkheer Van Tets (a red currant with large juicy berries)
White Versailles (a white currant with large sweet fruit)
Jostaberry (a prolific cropper, self-fertile and thornless)
Black Chokeberry – Viking (large juicy fruits)

Freeze

Fresh after removing stalks (open-freeze then bag up). The fruits can also be frozen as a purée after stewing, sieving and cooling.

Bottle

See Part One (pages 23-24) for methods. If heating in water, heat to simmering (88°C / 190°F) in 30 minutes and hold this for a further 2 minutes. If heating in the oven, keep at 150° / 300°FC for 40 minutes (for up to 2kg / 4½lb fruit) or for 60 minutes (for up to 5kg / 11lb fruit).

BLACK CURRANT JAM

2kg / 4½ lb black currants
2 litres / 4 pints water
3kg / 6lb 9 oz sugar

Wash the currants, heat with the water and simmer until tender.
Keep simmering and stirring until the pulp is thick then add the sugar.
Stir, boil, and keep boiling hard until setting point.
Jar up and seal.

BLACK CURRANT JELLY

2kg / 4½ lb black currants
1.5 litres / 3 pints water
Sugar

Simmer the washed fruit in the water until tender.
Mash the currants and strain before doing a pectin test (see pages
27-30 for details) and adding sugar (if high in pectin, allow 1kg /
2½ lb of sugar per litre of juice; if only moderate levels of pectin,
reduce to 600g / 1lb 5oz of sugar per litre of juice).
Bring back to the boil, then boil hard for ten minutes before testing
for setting point. When this has been reached, remove the pan from
the heat, skim off any scum from the surface, then ladle the jelly into
sterilised jars.
Cover and store.

BLACK CURRANT BUTTER

2kg / 4½ lb black currants
2 litres / 4 pints water
Sugar
2 teaspoons of ground cloves and cinnamon

Place the currants in a thick-bottomed pan with the water.
Bring to the boil, then simmer until the fruit is soft.
Push through a sieve and then put the pulp back in the pan and cook
slowly, stirring all the time, until the mixture is soft.
Add 500g / 1lb sugar per 1kg / 2½ lb of fruit, and the spices, then
boil until thick.
Pour into sterilised jars and top with lids or waxed discs and cellu-
lose as you would for jam.

BLACK CURRANT JUICE

Extract the juice using a fruit press or electric juicer. Freshly-pressed juice will keep only for a day or two in the fridge before fermenting – but don't forget to freeze some. This can be done in plastic bags inside small boxes (e.g. juice cartons) – when frozen the boxes can be removed and the blocks of juice packed together. Empty plastic milk cartons can also be used for freezing juice – but they must be thoroughly cleaned, and don't forget to leave 5cm / 2 inches space for expansion as the juice freezes. You may wish to dilute the juice for drinking, or try mixing with other juices – black currant and apple juice make a good combination for example.

BLACK CURRANT WINE

See Part One (pages 31-32) for general instructions.
Crush 1kg / *2lb 3 oz* of black currants and add 1kg / *2lb 3 oz* chopped sultanas, 2.5kg / 5½ lb sugar and the juice of a lemon.
Stir in 3 litres / 6 pints of boiling water.
Add yeast to the cooled liquid, and ferment.
When fermentation has ceased, rack the liquid into sterile bottles, cork and store somewhere cool and dark.

■　■　■

BROCCOLI AND CALABRESE

The big green heads you buy in the health food store – that are called 'broccoli' – are actually calabrese. Real broccoli varieties are generally the sort you can continually cut heads (or spears) from throughout the season – such as purple sprouting. By careful choice of different varieties – early-sprouting, late-sprouting and calabrese, for example – you can have fresh broccoli available for much of the year. Regular picking of the flowering heads will encourage side-shoots with new heads to form, and this will prolong the cropping season considerably.

Otherwise, all types of broccoli and calabrese are best stored by freezing. Harvest them before the tiny flowers open.

Recommended varieties

Rudolph (very early purple variety ready to crop from early winter)
White Sprouting (delicately flavoured white spears ready from March/April)
Spike (purple variety ready to crop from August)
Pacifica (calabrese type, ready in August)
Chevalier (calabrese type, ready from September onwards)
Romanesco (produces attractive pyramid-shaped, yellow-green heads)

Freeze

Blanch for 1 to 3 minutes depending on stem thickness (so sort them into batches of the same thickness first). Broccoli heads can often lock together as they freeze, resulting in one green block that you have to smash apart, so it is a good candidate for open-freezing first (after cooling). To cook from frozen, boil for about 5 minutes.

BROCCOLI SOUP

If you have an abundance of broccoli you can make larger quantities of this soup and freeze it in batches.
500g / 1lb broccoli
300g / 10oz potatoes
1 onion
1 tablespoon oil
1 litre / 2 pints stock
Salt and pepper

Chop the onion and fry in the oil in a large pan for five minutes.
Chop the broccoli heads and potatoes and add with the other ingredients to the pan, bring to the boil and simmer for 15 minutes.
Process with a blender and check the seasoning.
Add a spoon of cream to each bowl before serving if desired.

■ ■ ■

BRUSSELS SPROUTS

In recent years, F1 hybrids of Brussels sprouts have been developed – these have a compact growth and the tight 'button' sprouts all mature at the same time. They are fine if you have a freezer, and of course have been developed for growers who want to harvest all the sprouts at the same time for market, but many gardeners still grow the open-pollinated, conventional varieties. On these plants the sprouts mature a few at a time on each plant, so harvesting may be carried out over a period of months – ideal for those without a freezer, or those wishing to eat fresh sprouts direct from the garden.

Keep cutting Brussels sprouts while they are small – working up the stem of the plant – and you will be harvesting these from October to March. Freeze plenty for use throughout the rest of the year. Harvest only a few from each plant at a time. When all the sprouts are gone you can also use the top of the plant like a cabbage. Sprouts taste sweeter after the first frosts but early varieties can be grown for an end-of-summer harvest. If you are expecting very hard frosts, then you can pull up entire plants and hang in a cool frost-free building where the sprouts can be picked in fresh condition for a few weeks.

Recommended varieties

Oliver (harvest from August until October)
Maximus (harvest autumn onwards)
Darkmar (harvest from late November)
Trafalgar (top choice for Christmas – harvest from December to January)
Wellington (a late variety – harvest from December to March)

Freeze

Pick sprouts while they are small and remove the outer leaves. Blanch for 2 minutes before cooling and bagging-up. To cook from frozen, boil for about 7 minutes.

BRUSSELS SPROUT AND ONION SOUP

If you have an abundance of sprouts, all ready to harvest at the same time, you can make larger quantities of this soup and freeze it in batches.

500g / 1lb Brussels sprouts
500g / 1lb onions
1.5 litres / 3 pints stock
30g / 1oz butter
1 tablespoon sugar
Mixed herbs
Salt and pepper
Soured cream

Slice the onions and gently heat in the butter in a covered pan for 30 minutes. Uncover the pan, add the sugar and cook for a further 10 minutes to caramelise the onions.
Add the halved sprouts, herbs, stock, salt and pepper and stir well.
Bring to the boil and simmer for ten minutes.
Process with a blender and check the seasoning.
Add a spoon of cream to each bowl before serving if desired.

■ ■ ■

CABBAGES

There is a huge range of cabbage varieties available today, the vast majority of which are grown as annuals. Winter cabbages are best for dry storage but can also be left in the ground throughout the winter until required; red cabbages pickle well. This is another vegetable where use of a selection of varieties, which mature at different times of the year, will enable you to harvest fresh cabbages all year round. Sauerkraut (fermented cabbage) has been a staple dish in eastern Europe for centuries.

Recommended varieties

Spring Hero (harvest in May and June)
Advantage (harvest from June to November)

Stonehead (harvest from July to September)
Kilaton (harvest from October to November)
Marner Lagerrot (harvest from October to November, a red variety that stores well and is also suitable for pickling)
Celtic (harvest from December to February)
Holland Late Winter (harvest from November to December, a variety particularly recommended for sauerkraut)

Dry storage

Cut winter cabbages at the end of autumn, remove the outer leaves, and store nestled in straw or shredded paper in crates. They should be placed in a cool, dry building where the cabbages will stay in good condition until spring.

Freeze

Wash and shred before blanching for 1 minute, cooling and freezing in plastic bags. To cook from frozen, boil for about 5 minutes.

RED CABBAGE PICKLE

Shred the cabbage (usually a red variety is used for pickling), layer with salt and leave for 24 hours.
Rinse the salt off, pack into jars, and cover with vinegar.
Pickled cabbage can be used after a week and should be consumed within 3 months or it loses its crunch.

SAUERKRAUT

Finely chop 500g / 1lb of cabbage hearts, mix with 15g / ½ oz of salt and pack into large sterilised glass jars or a suitably sized plastic container.
Put a weighted saucer on top of the mixture and leave for a few weeks in a warm place (put the weight, if metal, in a plastic bag as it will become submerged in brine). As fermentation occurs, remove any surface scum every couple of days.
After about three to four weeks the sauerkraut is ready and can be used straight away. If you wish to preserve it for later use, strain the brine into a pan and bring to the boil, add the cabbage and return to the boil.
Then pack into warm jars and process in boiling water for half an hour (see Bottling on pages 23-24 for details).

■ ■ ■

CARROTS

The discovery of vitamins in the 19th century, and more particularly of vitamin A, increased the appreciation of the carrot in the everyday diet, as it could help prevent night blindness (it is true that carrots can help you see in the dark!). For this same reason, during the Second World War, British pilots were given large amounts of carrots in their diet.

If you are short of space in your freezer, just freeze the young tender carrots, putting the larger ones into dry storage or building clamps for larger quantities. Carrots also make a delicious wine.

Recommended varieties

Nantes 2 (an early variety, cropping from June, blunt-ended, almost no core, sweet flavour)
Chantenay (early maincrop, short wedge-shaped roots, rich colour, quick maturing and high-yielding)
St Valery (long slender roots with a yellow core, good for sandy soil, superb flavour)
Cubic (late maincrop, short tapered roots with deep colour, stores well)
Flakkee (a large carrot producing heavy conical roots which you can leave in the ground until needed – also stores well)

Freeze

Trim, wash and blanch for 4 minutes before cooling and freezing in plastic bags. Small ones can be frozen whole, large ones can be sliced or diced. To cook from frozen, boil for about 10 minutes or add direct to casseroles.

Dry storage

Leave until October then pull up and gently remove the soil from undamaged carrots. Trim off the foliage and pack in sand in boxes – in a cool, frost-free building they should keep until spring.

Clamp

Clamping can be a useful temporary technique for larger quantities. See Part One (pages 15-16) for details.

CARROT WINE

See Part One (pages 31-32) for general instructions.
Scrub and grate 5kg / 11 lb of carrots then boil with 2kg / 4½ lb of sugar in 5 litres / 10 pints of water.
Cool, add the yeast, and ferment.
When fermentation has ceased, rack the liquid into sterile bottles, cork and store somewhere cool and dark.

■ ■ ■

CAULIFLOWERS

Cut heads (also known as curds) of cauliflower can be hung in a cool building for several weeks before use. Freeze for longer storage, and don't forget to make some fabulous piccalilli (in which cauliflower is often the principle vegetable). There are summer, autumn and winter varieties of cauliflower available that mature at different times of the year. Most cauliflowers produce white or cream-coloured curds, but there are also green and purple-headed varieties available. Mini-cauliflowers, with a head about 5cm / 2 inches in diameter, are growing in popularity and are particularly suitable for freezing, but they must be picked at the point of maturity as they deteriorate quickly after this.

Recommended varieties

Médaillon (harvest from February to March)
Celebrity (harvest from April to May)
Candid Charm (harvest from June to August, freezes well)
Snowball (harvest from July to September)
Skywalker (harvest from August to October, freezes well)
Snowcap (harvest from November to December)
Minaret (a variety producing a green curd)
Rosalind (a variety producing a purple curd)

Freeze

Cut into florets and blanch for 2 minutes before cooling and freezing. Adding a little lemon juice to the blanching water will help the cauliflower keep its white colour. To cook from frozen, boil the florets for about 6 minutes.

PICCALILLI

2kg / 4½lb of mixed vegetables (cauliflower, marrow, small onions, gherkins for example)
10g / ¼oz turmeric
20g / ¾oz ground ginger
20g / ¾oz mustard
20g / ¾oz cornflour
200g / 7oz sugar
1.5 litres / 3 pints vinegar

Break the cauliflower into tiny florets, and cube the marrow and gherkins.
Peel the onions.
Soak all the vegetables in brine for 24 hours.
Put the sugar and spices in a pan and stir in the vinegar.
Add the vegetables, stir and heat to boiling. Simmer until the vegetables are tender but not pulped.
Add the cornflour (mixed in a little vinegar), stir and boil a further 3 minutes before jarring up and sealing.
Once opened, keep refrigerated.

■ ■ ■

CELERIAC

You can eat the leaves and roots of celeriac – both taste like celery – in fact it is also known as 'turnip-rooted celery'. The leaves can be used in salads or finely chopped as a garnish. The roots can be cooked or grated raw for use in salads. Unlike many other vegetables, the texture and flavour are just as good in large, older roots, so grow them as big as you like! Harvesting will start in October, but like some other roots they can be left in the ground until spring. If hard frosts are expected just cover the crowns with a thick layer of straw. The following storage techniques refer to the root.

Recommended varieties

Prinz (will tolerate light shade)
Brilliant (superb flavour, the roots store well)

Freeze

Wash, peel, cut the root into chunks and blanch for 4 minutes before cooling and open-freezing. These chunks are a great addition to soups and stews. They can also be frozen as a purée.

Dry storage

Leave until October or November then pull up and remove the soil from the roots. Trim off the foliage and pack in sand in boxes – in a cool, frost-free building they should keep until spring.

CELERIAC WINE

See Part One (pages 31-32) for general instructions.
Scrub and grate 3kg / 6lb 9oz of celeriac roots, boil with 2kg / 4½lb sugar in 5 litres / 10 pints water.
Cool, add the yeast, and ferment.
When fermentation has ceased, rack the liquid into sterile bottles, cork and store somewhere cool and dark.

CELERIAC SOUP

If you have an abundance of celeriac you can make larger quantities of this soup and freeze it in batches.
1 celeriac
500ml / 1 pint stock
250ml / 8 fl oz pints double cream
Herbs
Salt and pepper
Plain or Greek yoghurt

Peel and chop the celeriac and boil in water for 10 minutes.
Drain out the water, add the cream and herbs then process with a
food blender until smooth.
Add the stock and seasoning and reheat gently while stirring.
Add a spoonful of yoghurt to each bowl when serving.

■ ■ ■

CELERY

Celery can be left in the ground until it is needed. Frost protection is
rarely required, in fact there are some who say that the flavour
improves after the first frost. Celery is the ultimate slimmers' food as it
is said to burn more calories to eat and digest the stalks than there is in
the celery in the first place!

Harvested sticks will keep fresh in the fridge for some days, especially if stood upright in a mug of water.

Recommended varieties

Daybreak (early maturing for summer cropping)
Golden Self-blanching (cream-coloured flavoursome stalks, ready from
August)
Solid White (an old favourite, producing crisp, well-flavoured stems
ready from November)

Freeze

Wash well then cut into small chunks or slices. Blanch for 2 or 3 minutes, depending on chunk size, then cool and bag up before placing in
the freezer. Add frozen to stews.

Oregano hanging up to dry in the shed.

Rhubarb wine early in the fermenting stage.

Onions laid out on netting to dry in the sun.

Mixed herbs bottled after drying.

Red chillis drying before being stored in jars.

Open-freezing raspberries before packing in containers.

A variety of containers for use in the freezer.

Cabbage being packed into a pot whilst making sauerkraut.

Carrots stored in slightly damp sand in a cool building.

Oregano being dried in a warm oven for a few hours.

Gherkins pickled with a selections of herbs and spices.

Cider with an apple press suitable for home use.

Pumpkin soup – perfect for a winter's day.

French Beans dried prior to storage in jars.

Beetroot cooked and sliced before pickling.

CELERY SOUP

If you have an abundance of celery stalks you can make larger quantities of this soup and freeze it in batches.

200g / 7oz celery
200g / 7oz potato
1 onion
20g / ¾oz butter
1 tablespoon oil
1 litre / 2 pints stock
Salt and pepper
Parsley
2 tablespoons double cream

Fry the chopped onion and celery in a large pan with the butter and oil for 10 minutes. Add the stock and the diced potatoes, bring to the boil and simmer for 40 minutes. Process with a blender and stir in the cream.
Add salt and pepper to taste and garnish with chopped parsley.

■　■　■

CHARD

A type of leaf beet, often known as Swiss chard, though this is just one of a variety of chards – see also Perpetual Spinach (page 123), which is also a leaf beet rather than true annual spinach. With its brightly coloured stems, chard is attractive both in the garden and in salads. The leaves can also be eaten cooked in the same way as spinach. Chard can be frozen but with successional sowing and protection in the winter (cloches or similar will do) it can be harvested fresh from the garden all year round.

Recommended varieties

Rainbow Chard (red, orange, yellow and white stems make this one of the most stunning varieties to grow. Long growing season)
Swiss Chard (broad white stems and mid-ribs)
Canary Yellow (bright yellow ribs and stems)
Rhubarb Chard (tasty variety with bright red stems)

Freeze

Wash the leaves well, then blanch for 2 minutes. Cool and squeeze out excess water before freezing in plastic bags. It will freeze as a solid lump so fill each bag with only as much chard as you will need for one meal. To cook from frozen, boil for about 5 minutes.

■　■　■

CHERRIES

There are numerous differences between sweet cherries and acid cherries. Sweet varieties (of *Prunus avium*) are larger, suitable for eating raw, and are often self-sterile (so two different cultivars are required to produce a crop). Acid varieties (of *Prunus cerasus*) are smaller, used for cooking and making jams, and most cultivars are self-fertile.

In general, cherries are not very acidic, so are often mixed with other fruits for jam making, or used with the addition of lemon juice. Pick when they are ripe and of good colour, but not too soft. Use the best for freezing and bottling. Black cherries are the best for bottling or freezing as white or paler coloured varieties tend to discolour.

Recommended varieties

Early Rivers (an early, sweet cherry)
Merton Glory (mid-season, sweet variety)
Stella (a late, sweet cherry)

Morello (an acid variety with small fruits suitable for cooking or jam making)
Nabella (another acid variety with small fruits)

Freeze

Fresh after removing stones. Open-freeze then pack the fruits in plastic bags or containers.

Dry

Cut the fruit and remove the stones before drying them on a rack in an oven, drying box or food dehydrator. This can take up to one day depending on the method. Once the fruit feels dry and squeezing produces no juice, it can be jarred up and sealed. The product can be eaten dry as a snack or soaked for a day in water before adding to recipes.

Bottle

See Part One (pages 23-24) for methods. Cherries can be bottled with or without the stones. If heating in water, heat to simmering (88°C / 190°F) in 30 minutes and hold this for a further 10 minutes. If heating in the oven, keep at 150°C / 300°F for 50 minutes (for up to 2kg / 4½lb fruit) or for 70 minutes (for up to 5kg / 11lb fruit).

CHERRY JAM

4kg / 9lb stoned cherries
3kg / 6lb 9 oz sugar
4 lemons

Wash and stone the cherries.
Heat the fruit and stones (which contain pectin) with the juice of the lemons and simmer until tender.
Remove the stones, add the sugar, stir, boil, and keep boiling hard until setting point. Jar up and seal.
Note that Morello cherries are more acidic, so if you are using these, half the amount of lemon juice should be added.

■ ■ ■

CHICORY

There are two main types of chicory. Those that are forced (kept in the dark) produce heads (known as 'chicons') – these are grown from the cut roots of the plant in late autumn and should be harvested in the winter when about 15cm / 6 inches tall. Exposure to light will cause them to become too bitter so they should be frozen straight away, or kept in the dark and used as soon as possible. Non-forced varieties produce heads more like lettuce, which can be left *in situ* until needed. Using different varieties you can expect to harvest from June to October. In plastic bags in the fridge they will stay fresh for about 4 weeks.

Recommended varieties

Palla Rossa (a Radicchio type – the green leaves turn red in cold weather. Sow in spring for autumn use, or over winter to cut in spring)
Dura Witloof (grow in the dark to produce excellent chicons)
Pan di Zucchera (a sugarloaf type, producing tightly packed crisp leaves. Sow from spring to autumn and cut as required, can also be grown in the dark for chicons)

Freeze

Trim the heads of forced chicory and blanch for 3 minutes before freezing in plastic bags. Adding a good squeeze of lemon juice to the blanching water will help the chicons keep their white colour. To cook from frozen, boil for about 10 minutes.

■ ■ ■

CUCUMBERS

Cucumbers belong to the same family as melons, pumpkins, squashes etc., and it is the fruits that we eat. Early drawings of cucumbers show the fruits as being round or pear shaped, only more recent selective breeding producing the long thin fruits (for ease of slicing), the latest development (sadly) being the selection of straight cucumbers for ease of packing into boxes.

For centuries cucumbers have been eaten both fresh in salads and also pickled. Gherkins are merely varieties of cucumber that are harvested when small (7-10cm / 3-4 inches long) and pickled whole. They are usually of the ridge type that can be grown outdoors, and often have bumpy, or 'ridged' skin, and prickles.

Although cucumber seeds are soft, some people find them hard to digest, hence the production of 'burpless' varieties which have very tiny seeds (sometimes incorrectly called 'seedless'). If you do prefer to remove the seeds of your cucumbers, simply slice the fruit in half and scoop out the seeds with a teaspoon.

Wrapped in cling-film, cucumber will stay fresh in the fridge for a week or two. Freezing is not an option as the texture disintegrates. Keep harvesting the fruits before they grow too large – more will come!

Before the days of plastic-wrap, the skins of cucumbers were coated in a thin layer of wax, to slow down the evaporation of water. But even when waxed, they would only stay edible for a week or so and needed to be kept cool. Waxing is still used in some parts of the world. In fact it was the waxing that first led cucumbers to be peeled – but, as with many other fruits and vegetables, the skin contains flavour, fibre, and vitamins. So, if your cucumbers are organic, then do eat them unpeeled.

Recommended varieties

All the following can be grown outside, although they will do better in a frame, unheated greenhouse or polytunnel:

Tanja (produces long slim, smooth-skinned fruits in abundance, with no bitter taste)
Long Green Maraicher (another super variety grown for its taste and lack of bitterness)

Suyo Long (an unusual Chinese variety which produces long, thin, curled fruits with a ridged and prickled skin. The flesh however is tender and crisp and delicious)
Long White Paris (stubby white fruit – mild and attractive)

If you want to grow a gherkin variety specifically for pickling, then try:
Vert Petit de Paris (small, prolific and can be sown up to the middle of June)
West Indian Gherkin (egg-shaped fruits that hang on long stems like grapes)

Finally, for those who like to try something a little different:
African Horned (the short, fat fruits with big spikes are most unusual-looking, yet the flesh is juicy with no bitterness)

CUCUMBER JAM

1 kg / 2lb 3 oz peeled cucumber
1 kg / 2lb 3 oz sugar
2 tablespoons water
Juice of 2 lemons

Dice the cucumber and simmer in the water until soft.
Add the lemon juice and sugar, stir, boil, and keep boiling hard until setting point.
Jar up and seal.
An optional extra is to add a little ground ginger at the simmering stage.

CUCUMBER PICKLE

Small cucumbers or gherkins pickle well.
First, scrub gently with a scouring pad (which will also remove the tiny prickles) and dry.
Slice larger fruits or leave small ones whole according to your preference.
Then cover with salt, or a brine solution, for a day before rinsing, packing in jars and topping up with vinegar.
Seal and store in a dark place.
Don't forget the flavour improves after a few months.

ENDIVE

Endive is mainly used in salads but can also be cooked. Like lettuce, it does not store well, but as it can be kept in the ground and harvested throughout the winter this is not a problem. Successional sowing throughout the summer will provide harvestable endive heads until the next spring. It is a good idea to blanch the heads before harvesting to reduce the bitterness. This is NOT the same blanching you do before freezing – so turn the kettle off! In this case to blanch means 'to turn white' and you do this by covering the head of the plant with a pot to keep it in the dark. Begin this about 3 months after sowing, and harvest from a few days to up to a month later. Cut heads will stay fresh in plastic bags in the fridge for up to a week, but must be kept dark or they will become bitter.

Recommended varieties

Blonde Full Heart (large heads for spring and summer use)
Fine de Louvier (a tender variety with long serrated leaves)
Cornet de Bordeaux (dark-green crunchy leaves, harvest from November to January)
Pancalieri (sow from March to September for cropping throughout the year. Large heads with creamy-white hearts)

FENNEL

The feathery leaves of common fennel can be used for flavouring – with a strong aniseed taste – see Herbs (page 80) for storage techniques. As the leaves are very fine they are more suited to freezing than to drying. Florence fennel also has feathery leaves which taste of aniseed and can be treated in the same way. In addition, Florence fennel produces edible bulbs (swollen stem bases), also tasting of aniseed, which should be harvested when the size of a tennis ball in late summer. As it is a Mediterranean vegetable it should be sown in late spring when the soil has warmed up, or grown in a polytunnel, as otherwise it tends to bolt (flower and set seed).

Recommended varieties

Finale (excellent resistance to bolting so can be sown from March for an early crop June onwards)
Victorio (also has good resistance to bolting)
Romanesco (sow from May to July for large bulbs)

Dry storage

The cut bulbs of Florence fennel will keep for several weeks in a cool, dry place.

Freeze

Trim and cut into slices before blanching for 3 minutes. Cool then pack into plastic bags and place in the freezer. To cook from frozen, boil for about 8 minutes or add frozen to stews.

■ ■ ■

FIGS

Fig trees can be vigorous so it's often a good idea to restrict the roots, by planting in a barrel for example. The fruits, with a rich red flesh, can be eaten fresh or bottled, dried or made into jam for winter use. Ripe figs do not store well, so eat or process as soon as harvested or keep in the fridge for just a few days.

Recommended varieties

Brown Turkey (a hardy variety but for the best fruits grow in a greenhouse or polytunnel or against a warm wall)

Bottle

See Part One (pages 23-24) for methods. These fruits can be bottled either peeled or with the skins on as desired. Add a teaspoon of lemon juice per litre of syrup. If heating in water, heat to simmering (88°C / 190°F) in 30 minutes and hold this for a further 40 minutes. If heating in the oven, keep at 150°C / 300°F for 60 minutes (for up to 2kg / 4½lb fruit) or for 100 minutes (for up to 5kg / 11lb fruit).

Dry

Cut the figs in half and sprinkle with a little sugar before drying them on a rack in the oven, drying box or food dehydrator. This can take up to two days depending on the method. Once the fruit feels dry and squeezing produces no juice, it can be jarred up and sealed. The product can be eaten dry as a snack or soaked for a day in water before adding to recipes.

FIG JAM

1kg / 2lb 3 oz figs
1kg / 2lb 3 oz sugar
Juice of two lemons

Chop the figs and heat in the preserving pan with the sugar and lemon juice.
Stir, boil, and keep boiling hard until setting point.
Jar up and seal as for other jams.

■ ■ ■

GARLIC

Garlic is surprisingly easy to grow. It takes little space and little effort to produce enough strongly-flavoured bulbs to last you all year. Note that garlic you buy from the supermarket is unlikely to grow as well as varieties more suitable for a cooler climate – so buy a variety developed for cultivation in your region, and save a number of cloves each year for future sowing.

Recommended varieties

The following all store well:
Purple Moldovan (a heritage variety producing large, juicy, purple globes)
Thermidrome (large cloves, plant autumn to early winter)
Printanor (smaller cloves but store well, plant up until the end of February)

Dry storage

After the tops have died down in mid-summer, the garlic bulbs should be carefully lifted on a sunny day and left on the ground or on a wire rack to dry. The excess soil can then be gently brushed off and, when the skin on the bulbs is dry and papery, they can be stored in a cool, dry, frost-free place (not in the kitchen, or they will soon start to sprout).

Hang

They can be strung and hung like onions or simply left in boxes or hung in nets – see the Onions section (page 97) for instructions on how to string or plait the dried stems together, or just tie in a loose bunch. If the conditions are right they will stay in good condition for nearly a year – although some will start to sprout as the weather warms up again next spring. Either use these straight away or plant them for a late crop later in the year, but remember to plant a number of cloves in mid-autumn to late winter for your next summer crop.

■ ■ ■

GOOSEBERRIES

The name gooseberry or goosberry (which dates to at least the 15th century) is thought by some to come from the fact that the berries were commonly used to make a sauce for roast goose. Currants and gooseberries (*Ribes grossularia*) belong to the genus *Ribes* – and others believe that the French word for currant, 'Groseille', may have been mispronounced over time to arrive at the name 'gooseberry'.

Gooseberries are still used (as they were in the 17th century) as an accompaniment to meat dishes as well as a tart addition to poultry stuffing. More modern uses include gooseberries puréed with cream to make a frozen soufflé.

Gooseberries that are young and hard have a higher acid and pectin content so are better for jam making. Use older, softer ones for chutneys or wine.

Recommended varieties

Invicta (a well known heavy-cropper with a great flavour. The plant is resistant to mildew and produces large green smooth-skinned berries)
Greenfinch (high yields of exceptionally sweet fruit)
Pax (a sweet red dessert-type of gooseberry with large succulent fruit. Can be cooked, eaten fresh or used to make wine)

Freeze

Top and tail before freezing fresh in plastic bags. Gooseberries can also be frozen as a purée after stewing, sieving and cooling.

Bottle

See Part One (pages 23-24) for methods. Top and tail the gooseberries first. If heating in water, heat to simmering (88°C / 150°F) in 30 minutes and hold this for a further 2 minutes. If heating in the oven, keep at 150°C / 300°F for 40 minutes (for up to 2kg / 4½lb fruit) or for 60 minutes (for up to 5kg / 11lb fruit).

GOOSEBERRY JAM

2.5kg 5lb 8 oz gooseberries
1 litre / 2 pints water
3kg / 6lb 9 oz sugar

Wash and top and tail the gooseberries.
Heat with the water and simmer until tender.
Keep simmering and stirring until the pulp is thick, then add the sugar.
Stir, boil, and keep boiling hard until setting point.
Jar up and seal.

GOOSEBERRY JELLY

2kg / 4½lb gooseberries
1.5 litres / 3 pints of water
Sugar

Simmer the washed fruit in the water until tender.
Mash the berries and strain before doing a pectin test (see pages 27-30 for details) and adding sugar (if high in pectin allow 1kg / 2lb 3 oz of sugar per litre / pint of juice; if only moderate levels of pectin, reduce to 600g / 1lb 5 oz of sugar per litre / pint of juice).
Bring back to the boil, then boil hard for ten minutes before testing for setting point. When this has been reached, remove the pan from the heat, skim off any scum from the surface, then ladle the jelly into sterilised jars.
Cover and store.

GOOSEBERRY BUTTER

2 kg / 4½ lb gooseberries
500ml / 1 pint water
Sugar
2 teaspoons of ground cloves and cinnamon

Place the washed gooseberries in a thick-bottomed pan with the water.
Bring to the boil, then simmer until the fruit is soft.
Push through a sieve and then put the pulp back in the pan and cook slowly, stirring all the time, until the mixture is soft.
Add 750g / 1lb 10 oz sugar per 1kg / 2lb 3 oz of fruit and then boil until thick.
Pour into sterilised jars and top with lids or waxed discs and cellulose as you would for jam.

GOOSEBERRY CHUTNEY

2 kg / 4½ lb gooseberries
400g / 14 oz onions
20g / ¾ oz salt
sugar
400ml / 13.5 fl oz water
600ml / 20 fl oz vinegar
Spices of your choice (e.g. ginger, pepper, chillies)

Finely chop the gooseberries and onions and simmer in the water until very soft.
Add the vinegar, sugar, salt and spices then stir and simmer until a pulpy consistency is achieved.
Jar up and seal.

GOOSEBERRY WINE

See Part One (pages 31-32) for general instructions.
Add 5 litres / 10 pints of boiling water to 3kg / 6lb 9 oz gooseberries and 2 kg / 4½ lb sugar.
After 24 hours, add the yeast and ferment.
When fermentation has ceased, rack the liquid into sterile bottles, cork and store somewhere cool and dark.

■ ■ ■

GRAPES

Plenty of grape varieties are available, both white and black, for growing in cooler climates. Harvest the bunches by cutting them off with scissors when the grapes are ripe. To keep cut bunches of grapes fresh, cut them with a piece of branch attached – stick this in a jar of water and store in a cool dark cupboard for up to two months.

There is a variety of storage methods available – some obvious such as wine-making and others less well-known such as grape jam or ketchup – and do try making your own delicious raisins.

Recommended varieties

There many varieties available, some for outdoor growing, some more suitable for greenhouses; some for wine-making, some for eating as dessert. Here are just a few suggestions:

Boskoop Glory (a garden variety producing black dessert grapes)
Madelaine Sylvaner (early-ripening green grape for wine-making)
Black Hamburgh (for the greenhouse, producing large bunches of black grapes)
Foster's Seedling (an early variety of green grape for the greenhouse)
Black Corinth (small black grapes, but sweet, juicy and seedless)
Suffolk Pink (best in the greenhouse, this variety produces attractive pink grapes which are seedless and well flavoured)

Dry

For home-made raisins – only use seedless varieties. Dip the grapes into boiling water in a basket for a few seconds to break the skin then lay on a rack to dry in an oven, drying box or food dehydrator. This can take up to two days depending on the method. Once the fruit feels dry and squeezing produces no juice, the raisins can be jarred up and sealed.

Freeze

Fresh after removing stalks (and pips if desired) in plastic bags.

Juice

Extract the juice using a fruit press. Freshly pressed juice will keep only for a day or two in the fridge before fermenting – but don't forget to freeze some. This can be done in plastic bags inside small boxes (e.g. juice cartons) – when frozen the boxes can be removed and the blocks of juice packed together. Empty plastic milk cartons can also be used for freezing juice – but they must be thoroughly cleaned, and don't forget to leave 5cm / 2 inches space for expansion as the juice freezes.

GRAPE JAM

1kg / 2lb 3 oz green grapes
1kg / 2lb 3 oz sugar

Heat the grapes in the preserving pan to soften and then add the sugar. Stir, boil, and keep boiling hard until setting point.
Jar up and seal as for other jams.
If you are using black grapes you should also add the juice of three lemons.

GRAPE KETCHUP

2 kg / 4½ lb grapes
Spiced white vinegar
Sugar

Wash the grapes then simmer in a pan until soft.
Sieve the mixture and add 500ml / 1 pint of vinegar and 100g / 3½oz of sugar per litre of purée. Simmer until it has formed a thick cream then pour into warm glass bottles.
Top with an airtight lid and heat in a water bath at 77°C / 170°F for 30 minutes.
Tighten lid and store.
The sauce will store for several months and should be kept in a fridge once opened.

GRAPE WINE

See Part One (pages 31-32) for general instructions.

Ferment with the grape skins in for red wine, sieve the skins out and you get white wine – whether the grapes are red, black or green!

For every 10 litres / 20 pints of juice add 500g / 1lb sugar and the yeast before fermenting.

When fermentation has ceased, rack the liquid into sterile bottles, cork and store somewhere cool and dark.

■ ■ ■

HERBS

Pick herbs for storing on the morning of a dry day shortly before they flower. Choose the growing tips for the best flavour.

Recommended varieties

There are hundreds of different herbs and their varieties available – here are a few favourites:

Basil Sweet Genovese (large, strong-flavoured leaves)

Lemon Balm (lemon-flavoured leaves for tea, salads and in cooked dishes)

Chamomile Matricaria (dry the flowers for making chamomile tea)

Chives (easy to grow, edible leaves and attractive flowers)

Coriander (collect the dried seeds in August and use in pickling and cooking)

Coriander Cilantro (a variety of coriander suited for leaf production for use in salads and cooking)

Cumin (when brown, cut the plants and hang indoors to dry. Use the seeds for flavouring dishes)

Dill (both leaves and seeds can be used to flavour sauces, cheeses and pickles)

Marjoram Sweet (dry the leaves for winter use)

Peppermint (use to make mint sauce, tea and for flavouring dishes)

Rosemary (evergreen shrub with strongly flavoured leaves)
Sage (use the leaves fresh or dried for flavouring)
Tarragon (the flavour and texture of the leaves improves with age)
Thyme (low-growing evergreen plant with well-flavoured leaves for cooking or tea-making)

Freeze

A good way of keeping the flavour. The most useful method is to chop the herbs and freeze small amounts in ice-cube trays in water or vegetable cooking-oil. In each cube put about as much as you like to use in your favourite recipes. Either freeze each herb separately or make up your own mixtures. Once frozen, the cubes can be tipped into plastic bags and placed back in the freezer so you don't run out of cube trays. Label carefully as ice cubes containing green bits look remarkably similar. When needed, simply add a herby ice cube or two to your cooking. If frying, make it a herby oil cube! Large sprigs of herbs such as parsley, coriander and mint can simply be washed and frozen in plastic bags. They can then be crushed, straight from frozen, when required.

Dry

A warm, dry place is needed for drying. An airing cupboard may do but will take a few days – a warm oven (45°–55°C / 110°-130°F) will take a few hours. Herbs can be hung in bunches or laid out on a baking sheet. When the leaves are dry, crumble them into glass jars, seal, label and store in a cool, dark place. When using dried herbs in cooking remember they are stronger than when fresh.

If you are collecting the seed rather than the foliage – coriander for example – simply hang the whole plant to dry in a warm sunny room. Then shake the seeds off in a bag, and store in glass jars in a cool, dark place.

HERB VINEGARS AND OILS

Many herbs can be added to vinegars to impart their flavour. Flavoured vinegars can be used in salad dressings and to pickle other vegetables. To make a herb vinegar for salad dressings:

Crush a few leaves of the herb (or herbs) and add to a jar of wine vinegar or cider vinegar.
Keep in a warm place for a few weeks, shaking the jar every now and again.
Then strain out the leaves and use, or bottle, the vinegar.

Try it with thyme, rosemary, tarragon, basil, bay, dill or your other favourite herbs. The same technique can be used with oils like olive oil and sunflower oil to give them a particular herb flavour. The resulting oils are great for cooking with as well as for salad dressings.

MINT SAUCE

A large handful of mint leaves
250g / 8 oz sugar
400ml / 13½ fl oz malt vinegar

Wash the mint and chop very finely before distributing between a number of small glass jars.
Heat the vinegar and sugar in a pan until the sugar has dissolved then allow the mixture to cool.
Fill the jars with the vinegar mixture and seal immediately.
Store in the refrigerator once opened.

■ ■ ■

HORSERADISH

The young leaves of horseradish can be added to salads but the plant is most well-known for the sauce made from its roots. Traditionally this is used with roast beef but it also goes well with cheese. Dig some of the roots up in the autumn, they can be used fresh, dried or pickled.

Recommended variety

Horseradish (usually supplied as a bundle of roots, known as thongs, for planting in April)

Dry

Peel the roots and grate coarsely. Spread the gratings on a rack to dry in an oven, drying box or food dehydrator. Once it feels dry and squeezing produces no moisture, it can be jarred up and sealed.

Pickle

Peel the roots and grate coarsely, layer with salt and leave for 24 hours. Rinse the salt off, pack into jars, and cover with vinegar.
Pickled horseradish can be used after a week and should be consumed within 3 months.

HORSERADISH SAUCE

Large horseradish root or 2 small ones
2 tablespoons vinegar
1 teaspoon sugar
1 teaspoon mustard
200ml / 6 fl oz double cream (optional)
Salt and pepper

Peel and finely grate the horseradish before mixing with the other ingredients, adding the cream last. Whisk until the required stiffness is achieved then chill in a glass jar. Note that if you have added cream, the sauce should be used within a few days, but if the cream has been omitted, it will keep in the fridge for a few weeks.

■ ■ ■

KALE

Kale (also known as borecole) is one of the hardiest of vegetables – surviving the sharpest of frosts – so you can be harvesting the crop through winter to March or April with no need for protection. Due to its availability throughout the winter months, kale was sometimes the only green vegetable available to our cottage-dwelling ancestors. It was eaten day after day through the dark months, being added to stews or potage.

I often grow a plant or two in the greenhouse as well, for cropping an occasional handful of leaves from May onwards. It's very good for you too: the dark green colour is a clue that the leaves are full of iron and vitamin C. Old leaves can be bitter, so regularly harvest the young tender shoots. Once the plant has gone through the first frosts the bitterness will be reduced. Freezing the tender shoots ensures you have a year-round supply at your fingertips.

Recommended varieties

Red Winter (harvest from October to March, an attractive variety with purple stems)
Dwarf Green Curled (harvest from November to April, tightly curled leaves)
Pentland Brig (harvest from November, or sow in the greenhouse in March for harvesting leaves from May/June)

Freeze

Blanch the young shoots for 1 minute before cooling, chopping and bagging-up for freezing. You can open-freeze little piles of leaves or simply bag up portion sizes. To cook from frozen, boil for about 5 minutes.

KALE AND POTATO SOUP

500g / 1lb potatoes
250g / 8oz kale
1 garlic clove
1 onion
Olive oil
Seasoning

Peel and slice the potatoes, place them into a pan with a crushed garlic clove, a chopped onion, and salt and pepper.
Cover with plenty of water and simmer until the potatoes become tender (about twenty minutes).
Mash (or use a hand-held blender) until smooth. You may need to add more water to give it a soupy consistency.
Prepare the kale by chopping off the stalks and finely shredding the leaves.
Bring the soup back to the boil and then add the kale and simmer for around ten minutes.
Pour into bowls, adding a little olive oil (or cream, if preferred) to each bowl.
Serve with hunks of crusty bread.
You can also make this in larger batches for freezing portions.

■ ■ ■

KOHLRABI

A member of the cabbage family, kohlrabi grows fast and produces edible globes or swollen stem bases which should be harvested at about golf- to tennis-ball size within just a couple of months from sowing. They can be left in the ground until early winter but don't let the nutty-tasting globes grow too big. When lifted they will store for a few weeks in the fridge, or should be frozen straight away or packed into boxes of damp sand. The globes can be eaten cooked or raw. Kohlrabi leaves can be eaten too – treat them as you would cabbage.

Recommended varieties

Logo (quick-growing, producing white, flattened globes)
Azur Star (attractive purple bulbs with white flesh)
Superschmelz (this variety can be grown much larger without the crisp white flesh becoming stringy)

Dry storage

Pull up before heavy frosts threaten and gently remove the soil from undamaged roots. Leave a tuft of leaves on each bulb and pack in damp sand in boxes – store in a cool, frost-free building for up to two months.

Freeze

Trim, peel and chop into chunks before blanching for 2 minutes. Cool then open-freeze before bagging-up. To cook from frozen, boil for about 10 minutes or add some frozen chunks directly to stews. Alternatively the globes can be peeled, chopped and boiled for 20 minutes before mashing and freezing in a cooked state.

LEEKS

Leeks are extremely hardy and you should be harvesting them for six to eight months of the year: September to April.

Leeks can be left in the ground until they are required, otherwise freezing is really the only suitable storage method. They can be harvested at any size, the smaller ones having the greater flavour. You can also pull baby leeks in the early summer for use in salads.

Recommended varieties

Pandora (an early variety for harvesting from September, long uniform stems)

Hannibal (an early variety for harvesting from September, long thick shanks)

Bandit (a late variety for lifting in winter through to spring, high-yielding white stems)

St Victor (a late variety for lifting in winter through to spring, blue-purple leaves, stems have a good flavour)

Siegfried (a late variety for lifting in winter through to spring, produces giant stems)

Freeze

Top and tail and wash carefully to make sure there is no soil left between the layers of skin. Slice thickly and blanch for 3 minutes before cooling and bagging-up and freezing. To cook from frozen, boil for 8 minutes, or add the frozen slices to stews.

LEEK AND POTATO SOUP

The classic warming and comforting soup; cook in large batches, then freeze portions in containers.

4 leeks
6 potatoes
1 litre / 2 pints stock
2 tablespoons oil
Salt and pepper
Double cream

Wash and chop the leeks and potatoes and cook in the oil for about 10 minutes.
Add the stock, bring to the boil and simmer for 15 minutes.
Process with a food blender.
Season with salt and pepper and add a spoonful of cream to each bowl before serving, if desired.

■ ■ ■

LETTUCES

Lettuces come in a dazzling variety of textures and flavours, and many are highly attractive. It doesn't matter that they are hard to store, because different varieties can be grown year round, especially with the help of a polytunnel, cold frame or cloche, so your salad need never be without a selection of sumptuous leaves.

These days we recognise four main types of lettuce: Crisphead (Iceberg – e.g. Webb's Wonderful) which produce large crisp heads with solid hearts and few outer leaves; Cos (e.g. Little Gem) which produce crisp oval heads and are claimed to have a higher nutritional value than other lettuces; Butterhead (e.g. Tom Thumb) which are quick to mature and have a loose heart with soft leaves; and Loose Leaf (e.g. Lollo Rossa) which do not heart up and can be harvested a few leaves at a time – 'cut-and-come-again' – extending their productive season dramatically.

Lettuce will keep for up to a week in a plastic bag in the fridge, but better to leave it in the ground until the day it is needed. If possible, cut the heads in the morning for the crispest leaves. Otherwise the key is successional sowing, and to use different varieties that become ready at different times of the year. Lettuces cannot be frozen – the leaves disintegrate to a mush – and mid-winter varieties will have to be grown under heated glass. If you can do this, and also plant spring, summer and early winter crops, then you can have fresh lettuce from the garden for 12 months of the year.

Recommended varieties

There is a huge range of lettuces available. The following are just a few examples, some favourites and some for those who like to try something a little different:

Butterhead

Tom Thumb (a superb dwarf variety which grows quickly and is slow to bolt; one lettuce is just the right size for a salad for two)
Marvel of Four Seasons (red with curled leaves, not only does this variety look interesting and taste great, but it is also suitable for spring and autumn planting for eating throughout much of the year)

Cos

Rubens (this is a really striking looking lettuce with leaves of a deep red over dark green – good texture and flavour too)
Little Gem (compact and quick maturing with a sweet flavour. It can be sown from spring to early autumn and, under cover, can be eaten into the winter)

Crisphead

Roxette (a fast maturing variety with a solid heart and good flavour)
Embrace (this produces large, tight, crisp heads in a short period of time. It is an especially good crisphead for growing in unpredictable climates as sudden changes in temperature or rainfall won't split the heads).

Loose Leaf

Amorina (an extremely attractive variety with deep-red curly leaves. Cut a few leaves for a salad or cut the whole plant)
Belize (bright green, slightly bubbled leaves, forms a compact rounded shape)

Winter varieties

Winter Density (similar to Little Gem but with a larger head. Sow in autumn in the polytunnel or under cloches, and harvest through winter – slow to bolt)

Rouge d'Hiver (an old French variety with green leaves tinged with red. Upright with delicious leaves)

■ ■ ■

MEDLARS

Often planted for ornamental reasons, medlars are spreading trees with attractive foliage: pinky-green in the spring followed by rich red and brown autumn colours. The fruits are brown with five spikes on top (formed from the calyx) resembling a small crown. Pick the fruits in early November then leave them in a cool dry place for a few weeks until the flesh turns brown (they are unpalatable immediately after picking). They can then be consumed or made into jelly or cheese.

Recommended variety

Nottingham (a self-fertile variety which crops well and will grow to a height and spread of 6m)

MEDLAR JELLY

1 kg / 2 lb 3 oz medlars
250 ml / 8 fl oz water
Juice of a lemon
Sugar

Simmer the washed fruit in the water until tender.
Strain the pulp before doing a pectin test (see pages 27-30 for details) and adding sugar (if high in pectin, allow 1kg / 2 lb 3 oz of sugar per litre / 2 pints of juice; if only moderate levels of pectin, reduce to 600g / 1lb 5oz of sugar per litre / 2 pints of juice).

Add the lemon juice, bring back to the boil, then boil hard for ten minutes before testing for setting point.

When this has been reached, remove the pan from the heat, skim off any scum from the surface, then ladle the jelly into sterilised jars. Cover and store.

MEDLAR CHEESE

1kg / 2 lb 3 oz medlars
300ml / 10 fl oz water
2 lemons
Sugar

Cut the medlars and lemons into small pieces, and place in a thick-bottomed pan with the water.

Bring to the boil, then simmer until the fruit is soft.

Push through a sieve and then put the pulp back in the pan and cook slowly, stirring all the time, until the mixture is thick.

Add the same weight in sugar then boil until it is the required consistency.

Spoon into sterilised pots and top with lids or waxed discs and cellulose as you would for jam.

■ ■ ■

MELONS

Melons are climbing annuals which are usually grown in the greenhouse but can be planted outside in early summer in a sunny sheltered spot in warmer climates. String or canes can be used to support the plants, and when the fruits start to reach a certain size they will need to be supported in nets. They like a humid atmosphere so on hot sunny days leave a bucket of water in the greenhouse, or soak the path every morning. Once harvested, the fruits will keep fresh for several weeks if stored at temperatures of 10°-15°C / 50°-60°F.

The main types are: cantaloupe (thick, rough skins with deep grooves), winter (smooth yellow or striped skin) and musk (smaller with smooth skins such as honeydew)

Recommended varieties

Hale's Best Jumbo (tasty orange flesh, matures early)
Honeydew Green Flesh (pale yellow fruits with juicy light green flesh)
Sweetheart (popular variety, easy to grow)
Pastèque à confiture (attractive yellow and green striped fruits with a sweet, green flesh. A good variety for making jam)

MELON JAM

1kg / 2 lb 3 oz melon
1kg / 2 lb 3 oz sugar
Juice of 4 lemons
50g / 1½ oz crystallised ginger

Dice the melon and mix with the sugar and chopped ginger.
Leave overnight.
Simmer the mixture in the preserving pan, then add the lemon juice.
Stir and boil hard until setting point is reached.
Jar up and seal.

■ ■ ■

MULBERRIES

Mulberries are sweet loganberry-like fruits produced on medium-sized trees. Harvest the fruits in August and September. They can be eaten fresh or made into jams, wine or used in recipes in much the same way as loganberries or raspberries. Ensure the fruits used for jam making are very fresh.

Recommended varieties

Black Mulberry (a slow-growing tree with large juicy black fruits)
White Mulberry (a faster-growing tree with sweet fruits ranging in colour from white to pink to deep red)

Freeze

Fresh after removing stalks (open-freeze then bag up). They can also be frozen as a purée after stewing and sieving.

Bottle

See Part One (pages 23-24) for methods. If heating in water, heat to simmering (88°C / 190°F) in 30 minutes and hold this for a further 2 minutes. If heating in the oven, keep at 150°C / 300°F for 40 minutes (for up to 2kg / 4½lb fruit) or for 60 minutes (for up to 5kg / 11lb fruit).

MULBERRY JAM

1kg / 2lb 3 oz mulberries
1kg / 2lb 3 oz sugar
2 tablespoons water

Simmer the berries in the water until soft before adding the sugar.
Stir and boil hard until setting point is reached.
Jar up and seal.

MULBERRY JELLY

1kg / 2lb 3 oz mulberries
2 cooking apples
250ml / 8 fl oz water
Juice of a lemon
Sugar

Simmer the washed mulberries and chopped apples in the water until tender.
Strain the pulp before doing a pectin test (see pages 27-30 for details) and adding sugar (if high in pectin, allow 1kg / *2lb 3 oz* of sugar per litre of juice; if only moderate levels of pectin, reduce to 600g / 1lb 5oz of sugar per litre / pint of juice).
Add the lemon juice, bring back to the boil, then boil hard for ten minutes before testing for setting point.

When this has been reached, remove the pan from the heat, skim off any scum from the surface, then ladle the jelly into sterilised jars. Cover and store.

MULBERRY CHEESE

1kg / 2lb 3 oz mulberries
2 tablespoons water
Sugar

Simmer the berries in a thick-bottomed pan with the water until the fruit is soft.
Push through a sieve and then put the pulp back in the pan and cook slowly, stirring all the time, until the mixture is thick.
Add the same weight in sugar then boil until it is the required consistency.
Spoon into sterilised pots and top with lids or waxed discs and cellulose as you would for jam.

■ ■ ■

MUSHROOMS

If you are drying or freezing mushrooms, this must be done as soon as possible after picking. Pick by twisting rather than cutting the stems. Ideally mushrooms should not be washed or peeled – any dirt should just be wiped or brushed off the caps. If you need to keep them fresh in the fridge then a paper bag should be used – plastic bags just make them sweat and therefore disintegrate more quickly.

Recommended varieties

White Cap (grow on well-rotted horse manure throughout the year, or on a lawn in the spring)
Oyster (can be grown on logs or in straw – kits containing all you need are available)

Shiitake (available as inoculated logs)
Hericium (the fruiting bodies look like albino hedgehogs! Available as dowels for inoculating oak, beech or birch logs)

Dry

Slice the mushrooms then dry in a warm oven (45°-55°C / (110°-130°F) on a rack for a few hours. Large mushrooms can be sliced to speed up the process. A drying box or dehydrator can also be used with good results, or thread a string of small mushrooms on strong cotton and hang in a dry airy place for a few days. Store the dried mushrooms in an airtight jar in a cool, dark place – they are then a great addition to soups and stews. The drying process gives mushrooms new flavours and textures which are considered a delicacy by many.

Freeze

Button mushrooms can be frozen whole, or large ones can be sliced. If frozen raw they will keep well only for about a month; if first cooked by frying for a few minutes they will keep better – up to 3 months. Add frozen mushrooms to soups, stews, casseroles etc.

MUSHROOM PICKLE

Put clean mushrooms in a pan and cover with vinegar.
Season with salt, pepper and spice if desired.
Heat gently until the mushrooms have visibly shrunk, then jar up, covering with the hot vinegar.
Seal and store.

MUSHROOM KETCHUP

1kg / 2lb 3 oz mushrooms
50g / 1½ oz salt
400ml / 13.5 fl oz vinegar
1 teaspoon of peppercorns
1 teaspoon allspice
Half a teaspoon ginger
Half a teaspoon cinnamon

Break the mushrooms into pieces, sprinkle with the salt and leave overnight.
Rinse and mash the mushrooms then simmer in a pan with all the ingredients for 30 minutes.

Sieve the mixture and pour into warm glass bottles.
Top with an airtight lid and heat in a water bath at 77°C / 170°F for
30 minutes. Tighten lid and store.
The sauce will store for several months and should be kept in a
fridge once opened.

■ ■ ■

NUTS

Mature nuts will store in their shells for a few months if well dried.
Sweet chestnuts can be simply stored in boxes in a dry place. Most nuts
respond well to salting (see *Salted hazelnuts* below) and this can be
used for raw nuts, or after cooking in oil. Pickled walnuts are an
unusual delicacy often eaten with cheese.

Recommended varieties

Hazel Cosford (large oval thin-shelled nuts, with short husks, and
sweet flavour. Better pollination is achieved when two different varieties are planted)
Hazel Pearson's Prolific (Abundant crops of small to medium round
nuts of good flavour)
Almond Ingrid (a very reliable cropper producing well-flavoured good
quality nuts. Planting two different varieties will enhance crop size. Do
not plant near peaches as hybridisation may occur resulting in bitter
nuts)
Almond Robin (very hardy, producing large sweet nuts)
Walnut (stately self-fertile tree with yellow-green catkins in spring and
delicious deep-fissured nuts that are produced after six years)
Chestnut Sweet (large deciduous trees needing an open sunny position
to fruit well)

PICKLED WALNUTS

Pick the walnuts while still green in early summer before the shells have formed. Prick each walnut several times with a pin or fork and soak in brine for several days, then change the brine and soak several days further.

Then spread the nuts out on a tray and leave for a day or two until they have turned black.

Pack into jars and cover with vinegar. Leave for several months before using.

For sweet pickled walnuts, simply add 2 teaspoons of sugar to each jar and a combination of spices such as ginger, cinnamon, cloves, peppercorns and allspice.

SALTED HAZELNUTS

Hazelnuts do not store as well as some other nuts as they tend to shrivel in their shells, but they can be salted to store for longer periods.

Shell the nuts, rub the skins off and spread on a tray to dry in a cool oven for an hour or two.

Pack tightly in a jar with salt, finishing with a 1cm / ½ inch layer of salt then seal and store. Alternatively, the nuts can be cooked gently until golden brown in olive oil and then stored in airtight containers with a smaller quantity of salt (e.g. 2 tablespoons of salt and 5 tablespoons of oil for 500g / 1lb of hazelnuts).

■ ■ ■

OKRA

Okra can be grown quite successfully in a greenhouse or polytunnel. The plants produce edible pods called 'ladies' fingers' which can be used in curries, stews and stir-fries. Keep cutting the pods while young – 5-8cm / 2-3 inches long and bright green – and use or freeze them as soon as harvested. Okra leaves can also be cooked or eaten raw in salads and the seeds can be ground and roasted to be used as a caffeine-free substitute for coffee.

Recommended varieties

Clemsons Spineless (a prolific cropper producing bright green pods)
Burgundy Red (a vigorous plant producing stunning bright red pods)

Freeze

Trim off the stalks and blanch the pods whole for 2 minutes before cooling and freezing in plastic bags. To cook from frozen, boil for 5 minutes or add frozen to stews or curries. The pods can be sliced while still frozen.

OKRA PICKLE

First of all, each okra pod should be pricked a few times with a fork. Cover the pods in salt overnight then rinse and dry before placing in glass jars.
Make a pickling mixture by heating cider vinegar in a pan and adding 4 tablespoons of honey and 1 tablespoon of salt per litre / 2 pints of vinegar.
Stir until dissolved.
Fill the jars with the hot mixture to cover the pods, ensure there are no air bubbles, then seal.
The pickles will be ready to eat after a couple of weeks.

■ ■ ■

ONIONS

A most essential crop – and easy to store. Onions are of course a vital ingredient in most chutneys – see the various chutney recipes throughout Part Two. This humble vegetable was very likely a staple in the prehistoric diet. Botanists believe onions originated in central Asia and researchers agree that the onion has been cultivated for 5,000 years or more. 'Know your onions' was a term coined in the 1920s because there were so many varieties of onions which over the years never acquired standardised names from one region to another – 'knowing your onions' meant becoming familiar with the varieties that were grown and sold in the area where you lived. In later years the phrase became an expression used to describe a thorough knowledge of a subject.

After the tops have fully died down at the end of summer, onions should be lifted on a sunny day and left on the ground. They then need a week or two to dry. The easiest method is to lay them in trays (clean seed trays will do) which are left in the sun, but brought indoors if rain threatens.

Recommended varieties

The following are all varieties that store well:

Stuttgart Giant (heavy cropper with well-flavoured flat bulbs)

Sturon Globe (large globe-shaped bulbs with thick skin)

Stoccarde (heavy cropper with large flat bulbs)

Dorato di Parma (late-maturing with large golden bulbs)

Red Baron (attractive red onions but do not store as well as golden varieties)

Paris Silverskin (small white onions recommended for pickling)

Purplette (small red-skinned onions recommended for pickling)

Keepwell (a Japanese onion for sowing in August and harvesting in the early summer of the next year. They will keep well for several months after this, by which time you should have harvested your maincrop of golden onions)

Hang

When dry, the best specimens can be hung in nets or strung together. They will store well in a cool dry place until the end of spring. Before you string onions make sure that they have dried adequately.

There are various methods for stringing – here's a simple one which doesn't involve plaiting or complicated knots: to start your string, take four onions and tie the stalks together, then tie the knotted stalks to a piece of string. Hang this from the roof of your store and then add further onions, one at a time, by tying their stalks around the string and sliding them down to meet the others. Don't add so many that the string breaks!

Freeze

Skin, slice and blanch for 2 minutes before cooling and freezing. Small onions can be frozen whole. When needed add frozen to soups, stews etc.

ONION PICKLE

Peel small and medium-sized onions and soak in brine for a day, before drying (on kitchen paper) and covering in vinegar in suitable jars.

To avoid sour pickled onions, add a couple of tablespoons of sugar to each jar and mix well.

You can also add a variety of spices or a few fresh chilli peppers. Don't forget to leave the onions to mature before eating – see if you can resist them until Christmas.

■　■　■

PARSNIPS

There is some folklore about the ideal harvesting times for parsnips. One myth says that parsnips left in the ground over winter are poisonous, another says that harvesting parsnips before the first frost causes them to be poisonous. Neither is true, of course, but it is true that they are sweeter after frosting. Commercial farmers use the refrigerator to bring about the conversion of starch to sugar by harvesting the parsnips in late autumn and keeping them at around freezing point for about two weeks.

In the garden, parsnips can be left in the ground until they are needed. If there are still some left in the ground at the end of winter, they can be lifted then for storage. Parsnip seeds don't store too well, so you will get the best results buy buying (or saving) new seeds each year.

Recommended varieties

Turga (well-flavoured variety which, in deep soil, will grow to produce wide shoulders and a long tapering root)

Half Long Guernsey (an old variety – 1860 – with a smooth skin and a sweet flavour that produces medium-length tapered roots)

Tender & True (well worth trying for its superb flavour and large, long roots. It is also resistant to canker)

Freeze

Trim, peel, and cut into chunks before blanching for 3 minutes. Cool then place in plastic bags in the freezer. To cook from frozen, boil for about 10 minutes or add frozen chunks direct to soups or stews. Fresh parsnips can also be boiled, mashed and frozen in the cooked state. Try mixing roots in mashes – carrot and parsnip together for example.

Dry storage

Lift the parsnips and gently remove the soil from undamaged roots. Trim off the foliage and pack the roots in sand in boxes. Store in a cool, frost-free building.

Clamp

Can be a useful temporary technique for larger quantities. See 'Clamping' in Part One (pages 15-16) for details.

PARSNIP WINE

Parsnip wine has been a favourite for many years. See Part One (pages 31-32) for general instructions.

For each 2kg / 4½ lb of parsnips you will need to add 5 litres / 10 pints of water.

After boiling and pressing, add 1.5kg / 3½ lb sugar and the yeast, then ferment in a suitable vessel.

When fermentation has ceased, rack the liquid into sterile bottles, cork and store somewhere cool and dark.

SIMPLE ROOT SOUP

2 parsnips
2 onions
2 carrots
2 potatoes
1.5 litres / 3 pints stock
Oil or butter
Herbs
Salt and pepper

Take a large pan and fry a couple of chopped onions in oil or butter. When the onions are soft, add a couple of parsnips, a couple of carrots and a couple of potatoes – cut into small chunks.

Cover with the stock (vegetable or chicken stock, but even water or part water/part milk will do if you don't have any) and add salt, pepper and a handful of mixed herbs. Simmer until the roots are soft – at least half an hour.

Then blend the soup (a hand-held blender is ideal for this) until there are no big lumps left. At this stage taste the soup – it often needs more salt – and if too thick add some boiling water.

Serve hot with crusty bread.

Optional extras are a swirl of sour cream on the top and a sprinkle of chopped parsley or coriander. Make in large batches and freeze.

■ ■ ■

PEACHES, APRICOTS AND NECTARINES

Peaches, apricots and nectarine trees all have a chilling requirement (ideally about 30 days below 7°C / 44°F in a year) in order to fruit. They require a fairly dry sunny summer in order to crop well and in some areas more success will be had if they are grown under cover – fan-trained against a south-facing wall in a large glasshouse for example.

Time your picking of these fruit carefully: ripe but not too soft. Use the best for eating now, bottling and freezing, second-best for jam, and worst for chutney!

Recommended varieties

Peaches

Peregrine (a good cropper of large well-flavoured fruits. Can be grown under glass or against a warm wall)

Nectarines

Lord Napier (produces large juicy smooth-skinned fruits. Can be grown under glass or against a warm wall but needs a warmer position than peaches to grow good quality fruit)

Apricots

Moorpark (large juicy fruits produced August to September)
Tomcot (compact tree producing excellent juicy apricots. They bottle well, and any fruits too ripe for jam making can be made into chutney)

Dry

Cut the fruit in half and remove the stones before drying them on a rack in the oven, drying box or food dehydrator. This can take up to two days depending on the method. Once the fruit feels dry and squeezing produces no juice, it can be jarred up and sealed. The product can be eaten dry as a snack or soaked for a day in water before adding to recipes.

Freeze

Either fresh after peeling and removing stones, or after stewing and cooling.

Bottle

See Part One (pages 23-24) for methods. These fruits can be bottled with or without the stones as desired. If heating in water, heat to simmering (88°C / 190°F) in 30 minutes and hold this for a further 10 minutes. If heating in the oven, keep at 150°C / 300°F for 50 minutes (for up to 2kg / 4½lb fruit) or for 70 minutes (for up to 5kg / 11lb fruit).

APRICOT JAM

2.5kg / 5½lb apricots
2.5kg / 5½lb sugar
500ml / 1 pint water

Wash and halve the apricots and remove the stones. (Note that as most of the pectin is in the stones, it helps to cook a few stones in the mixture and remove these as you jar up).
Heat the apricots with the water and simmer until tender.
Add the sugar, stir, boil, and keep boiling hard to setting point.
Jar up and seal.

APRICOT BUTTER

2kg / 4½ lb apricots
200ml / 6 fl oz water
Juice of 2 lemons
Sugar
2 teaspoons ground cloves and cinnamon

Cut the fruit into small pieces, and place in a thick-bottomed pan with the water. Bring to the boil, then simmer until the fruit is soft. Push through a sieve and then put the pulp back in the pan and cook slowly with the lemon juice, stirring all the time, until the mixture is soft.
Add 500g / 1lb sugar per 1kg / 2 lb 3 oz of fruit and the spices, then boil until thick.
Pour into sterilised jars and top with lids or waxed discs and cellulose as you would for jam.

PEACH CHUTNEY

2kg / 4½ lb peaches
250g / 8oz raisins
2 crushed garlic cloves
Juice of 1 lemon
25g / 1oz salt
500g / 1lb sugar
1 green pepper seeded and chopped
1 litre / 2 pints of vinegar
Spices of your choice (e.g. ginger and cayenne)

Peel, stone and chop the peaches.
Place in a large pan with the other ingredients.
Heat gently, stir, and simmer until a pulpy consistency is achieved.
Jar up and seal.

PEARS

Pears do not store well. They don't make jam well either, unless mixed with other fruits, and go brown if frozen. The best bet is bottling and dry storage – although they won't keep as long as apples. If you have had success at cider-making you may wish to try brewing perry as an alternative.

Recommended varieties

Beth (medium-sized, well-flavoured fruit which turns yellow when ripe. An ideal garden pear)
Concorde (heavy cropper, sweet juicy fruits, good pollinator for other varieties)
Conference (heavy cropper, firm sweet fruits)
Williams' Bon Chrétien (a popular and hardy variety producing delicious and juicy fruits)
Sensation (an attractive tree with red foliage producing red fruits with juicy flesh)
Doyenne du Cornice (a good dessert variety suitable for bottling)
Green Horse (a variety particularly suitable for making perry)
Malvern Hills (a variety particularly suitable for making perry)
Merrylegs (a variety particularly suitable for making perry)

Dry storage

Use only perfect specimens, wrap in paper and place gently in crates or on shelves in a cool, frost-free, but not too dry place.

Bottle

See Part One (pages 23-24) for methods. Peel, halve and core the pears first. Keep under water with lemon juice added to prevent them turning brown before bottling. If heating in water, heat to simmering (88°C / 190°F) in 30 minutes and hold this for a further 40 minutes. If heating in the oven, keep at 150°C / 300°F for 70 minutes (for up to 2 kg / 4½ lb fruit) or for 90 minutes (for up to 5 kg / 11 lb fruit).

DRIED PEAR RINGS

Core the fruit and cut into rings about 5mm thick. Place for a few minutes in a mixture of 300ml / 10 fl oz water plus 150ml / 5 fl oz lemon juice and a teaspoon of sugar. Drain the rings before drying them on a rack in oven, drying box or food dehydrator. This can take up to one day depending on the method. Once the fruit feels dry and squeezing produces no juice, it can be jarred up and sealed. The product can be eaten dry as a snack or soaked for a day in water before adding to recipes.

PEAR JAM

Pears can be used instead of apples in a number of mixed-fruit jams.

PEAR JUICE

Extract the juice using a fruit press or electric juicer. Freshly-pressed juice will keep only for a day or two in the fridge before fermenting – but don't forget to freeze some. This can be done in plastic bags inside small boxes (e.g. juice cartons) – when frozen the boxes can be removed and the blocks of juice packed together. Empty plastic milk cartons can also be used for freezing juice – but they must be thoroughly cleaned, and don't forget to leave 5cm / 2 inches space for expansion as the juice freezes.

PEAR WINE

See Part One (pages 31-32) for general instructions.
Dissolve 2kg / 4½ lb sugar in 5 litres / 10 pints of boiling water.
Cool the liquid and add 5kg / 11 lb minced pears and the juice of a lemon.
Add the yeast and ferment in a suitable vessel.
When fermentation has ceased, rack the liquid into sterile bottles, cork and store somewhere cool and dark.

PERRY

This is the pear equivalent of cider and made in exactly the same way – see Cider under Apples (pages 35 and 37) for instructions. To make the best perry, however, you need to grow perry pear varieties such as Green Horse, Malvern Hills and Merrylegs.

■ ▪ ▪

PEAS

Peas are well known for deteriorating rapidly after picking – or at least for losing their sweetness. The sugar is converted to starch within minutes of harvesting, so only pick the pods when you are going to use or freeze the peas straight away. When picking, hold the plant stem with one hand while you pull the pods off with the other – otherwise you may break the stem.

Peas have been dried and stored in many parts of the world for centuries. They were then either ground and mixed with grain to make bread and cake, or soaked and added to stews. In the Middle Ages dried peas became a staple food of the European peasants; they were cheap and plentiful and made a filling wholesome meal the poor could afford. Commercially, today, only about 5% of all peas grown are sold fresh. More than half of all peas sold are canned and most of the rest are frozen.

Sowing a succession of varieties every few weeks will result in a long cropping season.

Recommended varieties

Feltham First (can be sown in October/November for an early June harvest)
Early Onward (sow in early spring, matures quickly)
Markana (heavy-yielding pea suitable for drying)
Waverex (a Petit Pois type, perfect for freezing)
Sugar Pea Norli (a classic mange-tout variety)
Sugar Snap (pick young and eat the plump pods whole, or leave to mature and shell)

Freeze

Pick while tender, shell and blanch for 1 minute before cooling, bagging-up and freezing. To cook from frozen, boil for about 5 minutes. Varieties where you eat also the pod – such as mange-tout and sugar snap – can be frozen whole or sliced, after blanching for 2 minutes and cooling.

Dry

Leave the pods on the plants until they have turned yellow, then cut the plant at ground level and hang indoors to dry completely. When the pods have become brittle, shell the peas and leave on trays for a few days. Then store in a cool dry place in airtight containers. Soak dried peas overnight before cooking.

PEA POD WINE

See Part One (pages 31-32) for general instructions.
Boil 3kg / 6lb 9 oz chopped pea pods with 5 litres / 10 pints of water and 1kg / 2lb 3 oz sugar.
When cool, add the yeast and ferment in a suitable vessel.
When fermentation has ceased, rack the liquid into sterile bottles, cork and store somewhere cool and dark.

■ ■ ■

PEPPERS (CAPSICUM AND CHILLI)

These are best grown in the greenhouse or polytunnel. Most peppers grow green fruits which gradually turn red if left on the plant in the sun – they can be harvested as desired (some people prefer the taste of green, some the taste of red, and some can't tell the difference). In general, the longer you leave the pods on the plant the sweeter capsicums become and the hotter chillies become. Both capsicums and chilli peppers will stay fresh for several weeks in the fridge. For longer-term use they can be dried, pickled, frozen or made into fabulous sauces. When handling hot chilli peppers take care not to touch your face as the juice will sting if the tiniest amount gets in your eyes.

Recommended varieties

Capsicums

Bendigo (small fruits ready from August)
Golden California Wonder (large green fruits becoming golden yellow, very sweet flavoured)
Jumbo (large square fruits becoming red)
Bell Boy (very productive deep green fruits)

Chilli peppers

Ring of Fire (long tapered peppers that turn bright red)
Early Jalapeno (produces small hot fruits, green turning red, heavy cropper)
Habanero (small fruits turn from green to orange – one of the hottest varieties)
Purple (conical fruits almost black in colour, extremely hot).

Dry

An effective way to store chillies for up to a year. Pods can be dried on a rack in the oven (60°C / 140°F for one day), a drying box for two days, or in a food dehydrator. A simpler technique is to hang the chilli pods in strings (tie clusters of three or four pods by the stems every few inches along a piece of string) in a dry airy place until the pods snap when you bend them. Once fully dry, chillies can be stored in glass jars in a dry dark place.

Freeze

Both capsicums and chilli peppers can be frozen for later use in casseroles, curries etc. First remove the stalks, then cut in half and scrape out the seeds and white pith. Blanch capsicums for 3 minutes, smaller chillies for 1 minute – bag up when cool and freeze.

PICKLED PEPPERS

All peppers can be pickled and make attractive and unusual gifts in glass jars.

Slice the peppers and remove the seeds then cover in vinegar and seal. Large juicy capsicums should be covered in salt for a day before pickling or can be roasted first for 30 minutes in a hot oven (230°C / 440°F).

Remove the charred skins before covering in vinegar.

If you use a mixture of different coloured peppers they can be packed in attractive layers or patterns in the jars. They will keep for up to a year.

RED PEPPER RELISH

8 red peppers
8 green peppers
8 onions
500ml / 1 pint vinegar
200g / 7oz sugar
50g / 2 oz salt

Finely chop the onions and peppers and discard the seeds.
Simmer in the vinegar with the other ingredients until soft.
Jar up and seal as you would for chutney.

SPITFIRE SAUCE

A hot sauce guaranteed to spice up any meal. The recipe originates from the West Indies but you can try making it with a variety of different chillies and spices according to your taste. Using habanero chilli peppers, for example, will give you an extremely hot sauce, but even the more common long tapered peppers produce a wonderful colourful sauce to be taken in small doses!
Multiply the following quantities depending on how much sauce you are making:

10-30 chillies depending on type and size (these can be fresh or dried)
1 green capsicum pepper
1 onion
2 garlic cloves
1 teaspoon sugar
1 teaspoon salt
150ml / 5 fl oz vinegar

Roughly chop the peppers (removing the seeds will produce a better flavour-to-heat ratio), onions and garlic and heat in a pan with the other ingredients for 30 minutes. Blend in a food processor before pouring into warmed glass bottles and sealing. Once opened, keep the sauce in a refrigerator.

PLUMS, DAMSONS AND GREENGAGES

All types of plum trees require plenty of sun and relatively little rain. There is a wide range of cultivars and rootstocks available to suit most situations. Some, such as Victoria plums, can form quite large trees, while others will be more suited to fan-training against a south-facing wall.

Most plums make good jam, while purple plums are best for freezing and chutneys. Pick when ripe but still hard. Damsons set well as jams but greengages will need lemon juice added.

Recommended varieties

Plums

Victoria Plum (popular variety with large juicy fruits. Heavy cropper)
Early Prolific (small purple plums which can be eaten fresh or made into delicious jam)
Marjorie's Seedling (A good cropper of large juicy blue-black plums which will keep fresh in the fridge for several weeks after picking)

Damsons

Merryweather Damson (blue-black fruits with a strong flavour. Good early cropper)

Greengages

Old Greengage (fruit has translucent flesh and excellent flavour)
Oullin's Golden Gage (a vigorous tree producing large sweet gages)

Freeze

Fresh after removing stones – or after stewing and cooling. You may also like to skin them first, or they can be easily skinned after freezing by immersing the frozen plums in hot water for a minute or two, after which the skins will slide off when the fruit is squeezed.

Dry

To create prunes! Cut the plums and remove the stones before drying them on a rack in the oven, drying box or food dehydrator. This can take up to two days depending on the method. Once the fruit feels dry and squeezing produces no juice, it can be jarred up and sealed. The product can be eaten dry as a snack or soaked for a day in water before adding to recipes.

Bottle

See Part One (pages 23-24) for methods. These fruits can be bottled with or without stones as desired. If heating in water, heat to simmering (88°C / 190°F) in 30 minutes and hold this for a further 10 minutes. If heating in the oven, keep at 150°C / 300°F for 50 minutes (for up to 2kg / 4½lb fruit) or for 70 minutes (for up to 5kg / 11lb fruit).

PLUM JAM

3kg / 6 lb 9 oz plums
1 litre / 2 pints water
3kg / 6 lb 9 oz sugar

Wash the plums, cut them in half and remove the stones. (Note that as most of the pectin is in the stones, it helps to cook a few stones in the mixture and remove these as you jar up).
Heat with the water and simmer until tender.
Keep simmering and stirring until the pulp is thick, then add the sugar.
Stir, boil, and keep boiling hard until setting point.
Jar up and seal.
See also Damson and Marrow Jam under Squashes (page 127)

DAMSON JELLY

3kg / 6 lb 9 oz damsons
2 litres / 4 pints of water
Sugar

Simmer the washed fruit in the water until tender.
Mash the damsons and strain before doing a pectin test (see pages 27-30 for details) and adding sugar (if high in pectin, allow 1kg / 2 lb 3 oz of sugar per litre of juice; if only moderate levels of pectin, reduce to 600g / 1lb 5oz of sugar per litre of juice).

Bring back to the boil, then boil hard for ten minutes before testing for setting point. When this has been reached, remove the pan from the heat, skim off any scum from the surface, then ladle the jelly into sterilised jars.

Cover and store.

PLUM CHUTNEY

1kg / 2lb 3 oz stoned plums
500g / 1lb apples
500g / 1lb onions
500g / 1lb raisins
25g / 1oz salt
200g / 7oz sugar
600ml / 1 pint vinegar
Spices of your choice (e.g. ginger, allspice, nutmeg, cloves)

Peel and finely chop the apples and onions and add to the plums in a large pan. Add the other ingredients, stir and simmer until a pulpy consistency is achieved.

Jar up and seal.

DAMSON CHEESE

2kg / 4½ lb damsons
200ml / 6 fl oz water
Sugar

Cut the fruit into small pieces, and place in a thick-bottomed pan with the water. Bring to the boil, then simmer until the fruit is soft. Push through a sieve and then put the pulp back in the pan and cook slowly, stirring all the time, until the mixture is thick.

Add the same weight in sugar then boil until it is the required consistency.

Spoon into sterilised pots and top with lids or waxed discs and cellulose as you would for jam.

GREENGAGE WINE

See Part One (pages 31-32) for general instructions.
Remove the stones from 3kg / 6 lb 9 oz of greengages and add 2kg / 4½ lb sugar and 5 litres / 10 pints boiling water.
Cool, add the yeast, and ferment in a suitable vessel.
When fermentation has ceased, rack the liquid into sterile bottles, cork and store somewhere cool and dark.

■   ■   ■

POTATOES

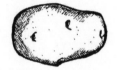

Like onions, potatoes are an essential crop: easy to grow and easy to store. Ironically, the dependable potato was responsible for one of the worst famines of the last 200 years. By the 1800s, Irish peasants were eating a daily average of ten potatoes per person – the potato supplying about 80% of the calories in their diet. They often ate them mashed with a little milk or butter. The peasants also used potato fodder to feed their animals which provided milk, meat and eggs. This dependence on one food crop was dangerous, but no other crop had ever proved to be as reliable. In the 1840s, disaster struck: three successive years of late blight and heavy rains rotted the potato crops in the ground. Without potatoes, both the peasants and animals went hungry. And when the animals died for lack of food, milk, meat and eggs were no longer available. More than one million of Ireland's eight million inhabitants died of starvation; almost two million emigrated. The population of Ireland was reduced by almost one quarter, and has never regained its former numbers. Today, scientists are constantly developing and studying new and different varieties to prevent a disaster like this from happening again, especially in Third World countries where the potato is, or could be, an important staple.

Once the foliage has died down at the end of summer, cut the stems off at ground level and remove them, but leave the tubers in the ground for a further week or two. Then carefully dig up the potatoes on a sunny day and leave on the surface to dry for a few hours. Throw away any green potatoes (which are a result of exposure to the sun whilst growing) as these are poisonous.

Recommended varieties

Earlies

Red Duke of York (deep-red-skinned with yellow flesh, less susceptible to disease than the old and well-known Duke of York, but retaining texture and flavour)
Orla (high resistance to blight, scab and blackleg, oval with yellow flesh)

Second earlies

Edzell Blue (a bluey-purple skin and white floury flesh)
Osprey (smooth white skin, good for chips and baking, resistant to scab)

Early maincrop

Sante (the most commonly grown variety on organic farms, resistant to eelworm and blight, yellow flesh)
Remarka (good all-round disease-resistance, high yields with large tubers good for baking)

Late maincrop

Appell (high blight-resistance and good yields of creamy-fleshed tubers)
Arran Victory (eye-catching purple/blue skin and white floury flesh, good yield and blight-resistance)

Dry storage

Once dry, the tubers can be stored in boxes or paper sacks in the dark in a dry building. They should keep in good condition until spring, but check regularly and remove any that are rotting.

Clamp

Potatoes are the classic roots for clamping. See 'Clamping' in Part One (pages 15-16) for details.

Freeze

Smaller, new potatoes can be frozen after blanching for 3 minutes and cooling. Or peel and slice into chips, blanch in oil, drain, cool and freeze in bags. Thaw chips before deep-frying. Potatoes can also be frozen after cooking – roast or mashed.

■ ■ ■

QUINCES

Quinces are small ornamental trees which produce large pink flowers in spring followed by shiny, pear-shaped yellow fruits which are very fragrant and store well. Allow the fruits to ripen on the tree, then, due to their strong aroma, store away from other fruits. Quinces have been used for many years to make jam, jelly and wine. The fruits are rich in pectin.

Recommended varieties

Vranja (produces well-flavoured juicy fruits)

QUINCE JAM

2kg / 4½ lb quinces
3kg / 6 lb 9 oz sugar
Juice of 2 lemons
2 litres / 4 pints water

Peel and core the quinces, then chop the fruit and place in a pan with the water. Gently simmer for about half an hour until tender.
Then add the sugar and lemon juice, stir, boil, and keep boiling hard until setting point.
Jar up and Seal.

QUINCE JELLY

2 kg / 4½ lb quinces
4 litres / 8 pints of water
Sugar

Simmer the washed and chopped fruit in the water until tender (about an hour).

Strain before doing a pectin test (see pages 27-30 for details) and adding sugar (if high in pectin, allow 1kg / 2 lb 3 oz of sugar per litre of juice; if only moderate levels of pectin, reduce to 600g / 1lb 5oz of sugar per litre of juice).

Bring back to the boil then boil hard for ten minutes before testing for setting point. When this has been reached, remove the pan from the heat, skim off any scum from the surface, then ladle the jelly into sterilised jars.

Cover and store.

QUINCE CHEESE

2 kg / 4½ lb quinces
200ml / 6 fl oz water
Sugar

Cut the fruit into small pieces, and place in a thick-bottomed pan with the water. Bring to the boil, then simmer until the fruit is soft. Push through a sieve and then put the pulp back in the pan and cook slowly, stirring all the time, until the mixture is thick.

Add the same weight in sugar, then boil until it is the required consistency.

Spoon into sterilised pots and top with lids or waxed discs and cellulose as you would for jam.

■ ■ ■

RADISHES

If you want to eat radishes all year round, you can achieve this with a selection of varieties that mature at different times of the year. They are easy to grow, but don't restrict yourself to salad use – winter radishes can be cooked or pickled. The small, fast-growing radishes used fresh in salads should be harvested just a few weeks after sowing and used straight away, but the larger winter-types can be stored in a number of ways, similar to other root vegetables.

Recommended varieties

Spring and summer use

Rudolph (round red roots that grow fast and crop early)
Giant of Sicily (large bright red roots from spring to autumn)
White Dream (long tapered white roots)
French Breakfast (a favourite variety, elongated red roots with a white tip)

Autumn and winter use

Sow July onwards for harvesting October onwards
Rosa (long tapered red roots with white flesh)
Minowase (long white roots – leave in the ground until required)
Black Spanish Round (round black-skinned roots with white flesh)

Dry storage

Trim off the foliage and pack in sand in boxes – in a cool, frost-free building they should keep for several months.

Clamp

Can be a useful temporary technique for larger quantities. See 'Clamping' in Part One (pages 15-16) for details.

RADISH PICKLE

Winter radishes can grow large, so best to scrub the skins clean and slice before layering with salt (or putting in brine) and leaving for 24 hours.
Rinse the salt off, pack into jars, and cover with vinegar.

■ ■ ■

RASPBERRIES, LOGANBERRIES, TAYBERRIES AND BOYSENBERRIES

The two main types of raspberries are those that fruit in the summer over a short season with heavy crops, and those that fruit over the autumn with a protracted cropping period until the first frosts. Loganberries, Tayberries and Boysenberries are all hybrid berries as a result of various crosses, and can all be treated in a similar way to raspberries as far as storage is concerned. There is a variety of suggestions below, but do experiment with any of these berries in each case.

All these fruits are excellent for jam making, bottling and freezing. Pick when large and well-coloured, before they go soft.

Recommended varieties

Raspberries
Malling Jewel (a favourite early variety producing juicy flavoursome fruit)
Glen Lyon (heavy cropping thornless variety which freezes well)
Octavia (summer cropping raspberry with sweet fruits)
Autumn Bliss (autumn variety cropping from August until first frosts. Suitable for freezing)

Loganberries
Thornless LY 654 (blackberry x raspberry hybrid. Good cropper of large well-flavoured loganberries)

Tayberries

Buckingham (blackberry x raspberry hybrid. A spineless variety producing enormous berries resembling loganberries of excellent sweet flavour. Suitable for dessert, jam making and freezing)

Boysenberries

Thornless (loganberry x blackberry x raspberry hybrid. Large dark purple fruits resembling raspberries with the flavour of wild blackberries. Delicious eaten raw or cooked)

Freeze

Fresh after removing stalks (open-freeze then bag up). They can also be frozen as a purée after stewing and sieving.

Bottle

See Part One (pages 23-24) for methods. If heating in water, heat to simmering (88° / 190°FC) in 30 minutes and hold this for a further 2 minutes. If heating in the oven, keep at 150°C / 300°F for 40 minutes (for up to 2kg / 4½lb fruit) or for 60 minutes (for up to 5kg / 11lb fruit).

RASPBERRY JAM

2kg / 4½lb raspberries
2kg / 4½lb sugar

Heat the raspberries and gently simmer until tender.
Add the sugar, stir, boil, and keep boiling hard until setting point.
Jar up and seal.
See also Rhubarb and Loganberry Jam under Rhubarb (page 121)

LOGANBERRY/RASPBERRY JELLY

3kg / 6lb 9oz berries
1 litre / 2 pints of water (omit the water if using raspberries)
Sugar

Simmer the washed fruit in the water until tender.
Mash the berries and strain before doing a pectin test (see pages 27-30 for details) and adding sugar (if high in pectin, allow 1kg / 2lb 3oz of sugar per litre / pint of juice; if only moderate levels of pectin reduce to 600g / 1lb 5oz of sugar per litre / pint of juice).
Bring back to the boil, then boil hard for ten minutes before testing

for setting point. When this has been reached, remove the pan from the heat, skim off any scum from the surface, then ladle the jelly into sterilised jars.

Cover and store.

LOGANBERRY WINE

See Part One (pages 31-32) for general instructions.

Mash 3 kg / 6 lb 3 oz of loganberries with 1 kg / 2 lb 3 oz sultanas.

Add 3 litres / 6.5 pints of boiling water and stir well.

Strain (ensure all the pips are removed), then add 2.5 kg / 5½ lb of sugar.

Cool, add the yeast, and ferment in a suitable vessel.

When fermentation has ceased, rack the liquid into sterile bottles, cork and store somewhere cool and dark.

■ ■ ■

RHUBARB

Rhubarb makes good jam, wine and chutneys. Use the young, spring shoots for freezing and bottling. The practice of 'forcing' rhubarb is often used for an early crop of tender, pale stems. The easiest way of doing this is to cover one or two crowns in January with a large pot, upturned dustbin or a special forcing pot. Check regularly for signs of shoots and cut as required. Established plants will crop for many years.

Recommended varieties

Champagne (an early variety often available as crowns)

Victoria (reliable cropper that forces well)

Glaskin's Perpetual (a quick-growing variety that can be grown from seed)

Freeze

Simply cut into chunks and open-freeze before bagging-up. Blanching for 1 minute will retain the colour, but it is not necessary.

Bottle

See Part One (pages 23-24) for methods. Cut the rhubarb into short chunks. If heating in water, heat to simmering (88°C / 190°F) in 30 minutes and hold this for a further 2 minutes. If heating in the oven, keep at 150°C / 300°F for 40 minutes (for up to 2kg / 4½lb fruit) or for 60 minutes (for up to 5kg / 11 lb fruit).

RHUBARB AND LOGANBERRY JAM

2kg / 4½ lb rhubarb
1kg / 2 lb 3 oz loganberries or raspberries
400ml / 13.5 fl oz water
3kg / 6 lb 9 oz sugar

Cut the rhubarb into chunks, heat in the water and simmer until tender.
Add the berries then simmer further until they are tender.
Then add the sugar, stir, boil, and keep boiling hard until setting point.
Jar up and seal.

RHUBARB CHEESE

2kg / 4½ lb rhubarb
Juice of 1 lemon
Sugar

Cut the rhubarb into small pieces, and place in a thick-bottomed pan with the lemon juice.
Bring to the boil, then simmer until the fruit is soft.
Push through a sieve and then put the pulp back in the pan and cook slowly, stirring all the time, until the mixture is thick.
Add the same weight in sugar, then boil until it is the required consistency.
Spoon into sterilised pots and top with lids or waxed discs and cellulose as you would for jam.

RHUBARB CHUTNEY

2kg / 4½ lb rhubarb
500g / 1lb onions
20g / ¾oz salt
1kg / 2 lb 3 oz sugar
1 litre / 2 pints vinegar
Spices of your choice (e.g. ginger, mixed spice)

Slice the rhubarb into short pieces and place with the finely-chopped onions, salt, sugar and spices in a pan.

Add half the vinegar and simmer the mixture until tender.

Then add the rest of the vinegar, stir and simmer until a pulpy consistency is achieved.

Jar up and seal.

RHUBARB WINE

See Part One (pages 31-32) for general instructions.

For each 10kg / 22 lb of rhubarb you will need to add 7 litres / 14 pints of water.

After soaking and mashing, add 1.5kg / 3½ lb sugar and the yeast.

Then ferment in a suitable vessel.

When fermentation has ceased, rack the liquid into sterile bottles, cork and store somewhere cool and dark.

■ ■ ■

SALSIFY AND SCORZONERA

These roots are hardy and can be left in the ground until required. Expect to harvest them from the end of October through to April. They can be treated like parsnips and are both delicious. It is worth lifting a few in early winter and putting into storage for use when the ground is too frozen to dig.

Salsify is also sometimes called 'oyster plant' as it is said that the white root tastes of oysters. The young shoots of the plant can also be eaten as a cooked leaf vegetable. The closely related scorzonera, which produces a long black root, is also known as black salsify or black oyster plant. The thick skin of the roots should not be eaten and can be removed either prior to or after boiling in water. If the skin is removed before boiling, the peeled root should be immediately immersed in water mixed with vinegar to prevent discolouration. The sap from the roots is very sticky, so it can be easier to peel after boiling for 20 minutes.

Recommended varieties

Salsify
Mammoth (long tapering white roots with a delicate flavour)

Scorzonera
Russian Giant (thin black roots with a delicious asparagus-like flavour)

Freeze

Peel, trim and cut into chunks before blanching for 4 minutes. Then cool, bag up and freeze. To cook from frozen, boil for about 10 minutes or add frozen chunks direct to soups or stews.

Dry storage

Lift in November, trim off the foliage and pack in sand in boxes – in a cool, frost-free building they should keep for several months.

■ ■ ■

SPINACH

By choosing the correct varieties you can have spinach ready for picking in the garden all year round. Perpetual spinach can withstand drier conditions than true spinach without bolting. Pick a few leaves from each plant, and use or freeze as soon as possible after harvesting. Wash the leaves very well in several changes of water to get rid of any soil. There's nothing worse than spinach that makes your teeth squeak!

Recommended varieties

Matador (slow to bolt, for spring to late autumn)
Giant American (large dark green leaves for summer and autumn use)
Giant Winter (very hardy, large fleshy leaves)
Perpetual Spinach (sow in April to July for harvesting from May to November, but as a biennial it will keep producing foliage into its second year)

Freeze

Wash the leaves well, then blanch for 2 minutes. Cool and squeeze out excess water before freezing in plastic bags. It will freeze as a solid lump so fill each bag with only as much spinach as you will need for one meal. To cook from frozen, boil for about 5 minutes.

SPINACH SOUP

If you have an abundance of spinach you can make larger quantities of this soup and freeze it in batches.

300g / 10.5oz spinach
100ml / 3 fl oz milk
2 tablespoons butter
Vegetable stock cube
Double cream
Salt and pepper

Wilt the washed spinach leaves in a pan for a couple of minutes. Add the butter and seasoning and heat through, then pour in the milk and crumble in the stock cube.
When it has just reached simmering point, remove from the heat and process the mixture with a food blender.
Stir a spoonful of cream into each bowl just before serving.

■ ■ ■

SQUASHES – SUMMER

Summer squashes, in general, are those which are harvested and used straight away in the summer, as opposed to other squashes like pumpkins which are grown and stored for winter use. Courgettes are, by far, the most commonly grown summer squash, and if left to grow larger will of course form marrows, which can be used straight away or left to store – so there is some crossover here between summer and winter squashes.

Courgettes belong to the family *cucurbitae*, along with cucumbers, pumpkins, melons, marrows and other squashes such as ornamental gourds. Archaeologists have traced their origins to Mexico, dating back from 7,000 to 5,500 BC, when they were an integral part of the ancient diet of maize, beans, and squashes.

As the plan is to use summer squashes straight away; they are not generally stored for long, although they can be frozen or pickled if required.

Recommended varieties

Courgettes

Nero di Milan (a classic dark-green courgette. An open plant so picking the fruits is easy)
Gold Bush (a yellow courgette variety originating from America. The bright yellow fruits have more of a buttery texture and a slightly different flavour from green varieties)
Albarello di Sarzana (a good-looking variety – pale-green mottled with yellow and a superb flavour)
Rondo di Nizza (green and round, if they're picked the size of a large orange they are ideal for stuffing)

'Patty pan'-type squashes

Custard White (flat, creamy white fruits)
Scallopini Yellow (bright yellow, very tasty fruits)

Freeze

Courgettes and other squashes can be frozen after washing, slicing thickly, blanching for 1 minute and cooling. To cook from frozen, boil for about 2 minutes or add frozen to stir-fries. They can lose their texture and become rather mushy after freezing.

COURGETTE PICKLE

Courgettes can be pickled in much the same way as gherkins.
Slice larger fruits or leave small ones whole according to your preference.
Then cover with salt, or a brine solution, for a day before packing in jars and topping up with vinegar.
Don't forget the flavour improves after a few months.

SQUASHES – WINTER

Marrows, pumpkins and winter squashes should be left on the plants until the first frost is expected. Then cut and store in a cool dry building – either hung in nets or placed on shelves. They will stay in good condition until mid-winter.

Although pumpkins and other squashes are 90% water, they have a lot going for them. They are good sources of potassium and Vitamin A with a sweet nutritious flesh. The seeds can be roasted as a tasty snack or used in baking breads and cakes. The flowers can also be used like others of the squash family: batter-dipping and frying them for example.

Marrows can be made into wine and jam, and flesh from marrows, pumpkins and other squashes can be used to add bulk and texture to all sorts of chutneys. Pumpkins make great soup and pies, butternut and other winter squashes also make good soup and are delicious when roasted.

Recommended varieties

Rouge Vif d'Etampes (a pumpkin with lobed fruits which have a good colour and mature quickly)

Small Sugar (a commonly grown pumpkin for making pies. Expect 2kg / 4½ lb fruits with bright orange flesh)

Pepita (produces attractive medium-sized fruits with green and white stripes)

Cobnut (a butternut type which matures earlier than other varieties)

Turk's Turban (often grown ornamentally but the pale yellow flesh is very tasty)

Tancheese (small squashes with a sweet, smooth flesh)

Blue Kuri (blue-grey fruits with bright orange flesh)

Badger Cross (tasty stripy marrows)

Minipak (small striped marrows, very productive)

DAMSON AND MARROW JAM

2 kg / 4½ lb damsons
2 kg / 4½ lb marrow cubes
750 ml / 1½ pints water
4 kg / 9 lb sugar

Heat the damsons with half the water and simmer until tender.
Sieve to remove the stones.
Simmer the marrow cubes with the rest of the water until pulped.
Mix the pulps, bring back to a simmer, then add the sugar.
Stir, boil, and keep boiling hard until setting point.
Jar up and seal.

MARROW BUTTER

Marrow
Sugar
Ground cloves and cinnamon

Chop the marrow flesh and place in a thick-bottomed pan.
Bring to the boil, then simmer until the fruit is soft.
Push through a sieve and then put the pulp back in the pan and cook
slowly, stirring all the time, until the mixture is soft.
Add 500g / 1lb sugar per 1kg / 2lb 3oz of fruit and a teaspoon of
the spices then boil until thick. Pour into sterilised jars and top with
lids or waxed discs and cellulose as you would for jam.

MARROW AND APPLE CHUTNEY

2 kg / 4½ lb marrow
1 kg / 2 lb 3 oz apples
500g / 1lb onions
75g / 2½ oz salt
500g / 1lb sugar
2 litres / 4 pints vinegar
Spices of your choice (e.g. ginger, pepper, chillies)

Peel the marrow and cut the flesh into small cubes.
Cover with salt overnight then rinse.
Put the marrow in a large pan with the finely-chopped onions and
apples and the spices. Heat gently and simmer until tender.
Add the vinegar and sugar, stir and simmer until it reaches a pulpy
consistency. Jar up and seal.

PUMPKIN SOUP

1 pumpkin
2 onions
Butter
Stock or water and milk
Herbs
Salt and pepper

Take a large pan and fry a couple of large onions in butter.

When the onions are soft add the roughly chopped flesh scooped out of the pumpkin (you need pretty strong metal spoons to do the scooping).

Stir this around and add a litre or two (depending on size of pan and amount of flesh) of stock or water and milk to just cover the flesh.

Season with salt, pepper and a good spoonful of mixed herbs.

Bring to the boil and simmer for at least 30 minutes until the flesh is soft.

Then blend the soup (a hand-held blender is ideal for this) until there are no big lumps of flesh left. At this stage taste the soup – it often needs more salt – and if too thick add some boiling water.

Serve hot with crusty bread.

Optional extras are a swirl of sour cream on the top and a sprinkle of chopped parsley. Make a huge vat of this soup and freeze portions.

MARROW WINE

See Part One (pages 31-32) for general instructions.

Add 5 litres / 10 pints of boiling water to 3kg / 6 lb 9 oz chopped, ripe marrow and 2kg / 4½ lb sugar.

After 24 hours add the yeast and ferment in a suitable vessel.

When fermentation has ceased, rack the liquid into sterile bottles, cork and store somewhere cool and dark.

■ ■ ■

STRAWBERRIES

Originally strawberries were called 'strewberries', because the berries appeared to be strewn among the leaves, and the runners themselves appeared to be strewn among the plants. Dr William Butler, the 17th-century English writer, was referring to strawberries when he said "Doubtless God could have made a better berry, but doubtless God never did." Yet he certainly wasn't the first to worship this most delicious of fruits.

The ancient Romans were the first to be known for preserving strawberries by pickling them. If you have more strawberries than you can eat fresh, straight from the plant, there are a number of ways you can store or preserve them for future use. Smaller strawberries can be frozen by open-freezing on trays before packing into plastic bags or containers. They can also be frozen as a purée after processing.

Strawberry jam is always a favourite and a great way of preserving larger fruits, but they can also be bottled and made into wine.

Recommended varieties

Honeoye (an early variety with good-flavoured red/orange fruits which do not split in wet weather)

Pegasus (mid-season. Strong plants producing large juicy fruits that store well)

Florence (a late season variety producing high yields of good fruits which are resistant to mildew, wilt and crown rot)

Symphony (late season with high yields of excellent-flavoured fruits resistant to red-core)

Freeze

Open-freeze before packing into plastic bags or containers. They can also be frozen as a purée after processing.

Dry

Cut the fruit in slices before drying them on a rack in oven, drying box or food dehydrator. This can take up to 12 hours depending on the method. Once the fruit feels dry and squeezing produces no juice, it can be jarred up and sealed. The product can be eaten dry as a snack or soaked for a day in water before adding to recipes.

Bottle

See Part One (pages 23-24) for methods. Halve and wash the strawberries first. If heating in water, heat to simmering (88°C / 190°F) in 30 minutes and hold this for a further 2 minutes. If heating in the oven, keep at 150°C / 300°F for 40 minutes (for up to 2kg / 4½ lb fruit) or for 60 minutes (for up to 5kg / 11 lb fruit).

STRAWBERRY JAM

2kg / 4½ lb strawberries
1 lemon
1.75kg / 4 lb sugar

Heat the strawberries with the juice of the lemon, stir and gently simmer until tender. Add the sugar, stir, boil, and keep boiling hard until setting point.
Jar up and seal.
If you have trouble getting your strawberry jam to set, try adding commercially available pectin.

STRAWBERRY WINE

See Part One (pages 31-32) for general instructions.
Wash 2kg / 4½ lb of sound strawberries and add to 2kg / 4½ lb sugar and 4 litres / 8 pints of boiling water. Stir and mash the fruit well.
Cool, add the yeast, and ferment in a suitable vessel.
When fermentation has ceased, rack the liquid into sterile bottles, cork and store somewhere cool and dark.

■ ■ ■

SWEDES

Also known as rutabaga, swedish turnip or yellow turnip, swedes were originally produced by crossing cabbages with white turnips. Swedes can be dug up as soon as they are large enough to use. They are very hardy and can be left in the soil until required. Expect to be harvesting from September to March. The new shoots in spring can also be eaten like cabbage. The yellow flesh from swedes is often mashed with carrots as an accompaniment to a roast meal. Mashed swedes are also known as 'neeps' in the Scottish 'neeps and tatties' (mashed swedes and potatoes often served with haggis).

Recommended varieties

Joan (sow from February for an early crop of small roots)
Airlie (medium-sized sweet-flavoured roots)
Wilhelmsburger (roots have a green rather than purple top, stores well)

Freeze

Wash, trim and cut into chunks before blanching for 3 minutes. Cool and freeze in plastic bags. To cook from frozen, boil for about 8 minutes.

Dry storage

Pull up and gently remove the soil from undamaged roots. Twist off the foliage and pack the roots in sand in boxes – store in a cool, frost-free building.

Clamp

If you have a lot of swedes, you can store them in a clamp (where they will keep better than turnips). See Part One (pages 15-16) for the method.

■ ■ ■

SWEET CORN (MAIZE)

Also known as maize or corn-on-the-cob. Like peas, sweetcorn loses its sweetness rapidly from the moment the cobs are picked, as the sugar is converted to starch within minutes of harvesting. So pick the cobs only when you are going to eat or freeze them straight away. If you have to store cobs for a few days, keep them refrigerated. An alternative is to grow baby corn; harvested up to 10cm / 4 inches long they can be eaten raw or lightly boiled and also freeze well.

Sweet corn can also be dried for storage and later rehydration or for making into popcorn, or can be bottled, or made into a tasty relish.

Recommended varieties
Sweet Nugget (grows well in a cool climate)
Swift (early maturing and freezes well)
Double Standard (produces white and yellow kernels on the same cobs)
Minipop (harvest small for perfect baby corns)

Freeze
Pull off the outer leaves and silks, trim the stalk, and blanch for 5 minutes. After cooling, wrap each cob in foil or cling-film before placing in the freezer. Thaw before cooking in boiling water for 5 minutes, or from frozen, for 10 minutes.
Alternatively, the corn kernels can be stripped from the cob using a knife, and then blanched for 1 minute before cooling, bagging-up and freezing. Baby corn will also only need blanching for 1 minute before cooling, bagging-up and freezing.

Dry
Leave the cobs on the plant longer than usual until the kernels start to dry, then hang them up indoors for a few weeks until fully dry. The kernels can then be stripped from the cobs and stored in airtight jars, until needed for popping or soaking before adding to soups and stews. Note that for successful popcorn the kernels must be completely dry.

Bottle

See Part One (pages 23-24) for methods. Strip the kernels from the cobs with a knife directly after harvesting. If heating in water, heat to simmering (88°C / 190°F) in 30 minutes and hold this for a further 2 minutes. If heating in the oven, keep at 150°C / 300°F for 50 minutes (for up to 2kg / 4½lb fruit).

SWEETCORN RELISH

6 corn cobs
Half a white cabbage
2 onions
2 red or green capsicum peppers
2 teaspoons salt
2 teaspoons flour
Half a teaspoon turmeric
200g / 7oz sugar
2 teaspoons mustard
600ml / 1 pint vinegar

Boil the cobs for five minutes before stripping off the kernels.
Add these to the finely chopped onions, cabbage and peppers, and heat in a large saucepan.
Mix the remaining ingredients into the vinegar and stir this into the pan. Bring to the boil and simmer for 30 minutes before jarring up and sealing in hot, sterilised jars.
This relish will improve in flavour if left for a month or two before opening.

■　■　■

TOMATOES

In many parts of the world more tomatoes are eaten than any other single fruit or vegetable. More than 60 million tons of tomatoes are produced per year. Part of the reason for their popularity is their versatility – not only are they an essential constituent of most salads, but as a sauce they are the basis of many meals: pizzas, chillies, curries, soups, pasta sauces and so on. And don't forget ketchup!

Commercially, tomatoes are picked green, and can be encouraged to ripen after shipping by spraying with ethylene which can affect the flavour (along with other chemicals that may have been used while they are grown). If you, like me, don't like the sound of this, then grow your own – organically.

Tomato plants are naturally self-pollinating, and a general characteristic of self-pollinating plants is that they become genetically similar after many generations. Early cultivars did not change much because of this property, and were kept in a family or community for long periods of time, thus earning the name heirlooms. Heirloom cultivars dating back over a hundred years are still grown today. Most heirloom varieties are unique in size, shape or colour. Varying from black, dark purple, or red with black shoulders, green, rainbow-coloured, or shaped like peppers. There are orange and yellow cultivars too, and everything in between. Some fruits are cherry-size, some are over 1 kg / 2 lb 3 oz.

Fresh tomatoes will stay in good condition for a week or more. Pick when ripe with a deep colour. Green tomatoes make a great chutney, or can be encouraged to ripen by placing them in a plastic bag in a warm room with a couple of ripe tomatoes, apples or a banana.

Recommended varieties

There are many varieties available, the following are just a few favourites as suggestions:

Red Pear (a smaller variety producing clusters of attractive pear-shaped fruits with thin skins)

Gardener's Delight (a favourite sweet cherry tomato with long trusses of fruits)

Lily of the Valley (numerous fruits hang on the stem like blooms of lilies of the valley)

Alicante (a medium-sized tomato with good resistance to mildew and greenback. An early cropper with good flavour)

Andine Comue (introduced from the Andes recently, this variety produces pepper-shaped fruits – early ripening and great for soups and sauces)

Potiron Ecarlate (a very large variety – for stuffing or slicing in salads or on pizzas. They taste great and the fruits can reach up to 1.2 kg / 2½ lb – each!)

Freeze

The easiest way is just to put them whole into the freezer. They can easily be skinned after freezing by immersing the frozen tomatoes in hot water for a minute or two, after which the skins will slide off when the fruit is squeezed. Then add to stews etc.

They can also be frozen after stewing to a purée, for use as a base for pasta sauces etc. Simmer for 5 minutes then sieve before cooling and freezing in a plastic container.

Dry

Tomatoes can be fully dried and stored in jars, or partly dried and stored in oil. Cut the tomatoes in half, lay on a drying rack in a low oven or in a drying box, and sprinkle a little salt on the upturned face of each half. The drying process can take up to a day depending on the size of the tomatoes – remove them when they feel firm and dry. For oil storage, remove them while still a little squishy and pack into sterilised jars, covering with olive oil and sealing. Either way they will store for up to 6 months. A food dehydrator can also be used – follow the manufacturer's instructions.

Bottle

See Part One (pages 23-24) for methods. First remove the skins of the tomatoes by scalding. Pack tightly and add a teaspoon of salt and a squeeze of lemon juice to each jar. If heating in water, heat to simmering (88°C / 190°F) in 30 minutes and hold this for a further 50 minutes. If heating in the oven, keep at 150°C / 300°F for 80 minutes (for up to 2kg / 4½ lb fruit) or for 100 minutes (for up to 5kg / 11½ lb fruit). The tomatoes can also be bottled as passata by sieving out the pips and blending with a food processor until smooth before bottling.

GREEN TOMATO CHUTNEY

2kg / 4½ lb green tomatoes
500g / 1lb apples
500g / 1lb onions
250g / 9oz raisins
25g / 1oz salt
500g / 1lb sugar
600ml / 1 pint vinegar
Spices of your choice (e.g. ginger, pepper, chillies)

Finely chop the tomatoes, apples and onions and place all the ingredients in a large pan. Heat gently, stir, and simmer until a pulpy consistency is achieved. Jar up and seal.

TOMATO JELLY

2 kg / 4½ lb tomatoes
750 ml / 1½ pints water
250 ml / ½ pint vinegar
2 kg / 4½ lb sugar
Optional spices such as cloves and cinnamon

Simmer the washed and chopped tomatoes in the water until tender. Strain before adding the sugar and vinegar.
Bring back to the boil, then boil hard for ten minutes before testing for setting point. When this has been reached, remove the pan from the heat, skim off any scum from the surface, then ladle the jelly into sterilised jars.
Cover and store.

TOMATO BUTTER

1 kg / 2 lb 3 oz tomatoes
Juice of two lemons
750 g / 1 lb 10 oz sugar per kg / 2 lbs of tomatoes
2 teaspoons allspice

Place the chopped tomatoes in a thick-bottomed pan with the lemon juice.
Bring to the boil, then simmer until the fruit is soft.
Push through a sieve and then put the pulp back in the pan and cook slowly, stirring all the time, until the mixture is soft.
Add sugar and spices then boil until thick.
Pour into sterilised jars and top with lids or waxed discs and cellulose as you would for jam.

TOMATO KETCHUP

2kg / 4½lb tomatoes
200g / 7oz sugar
450ml / 15 fl oz spiced vinegar
Large onion
2 large apples
Salt to taste

Chop the tomatoes and add to the peeled and chopped onion and apples.

Stir in a pan and cook until a thick pulp is achieved.

Sieve the mixture and add to the vinegar and sugar.

Simmer until thick and creamy then add salt to taste before pouring into warm glass bottles.

Top with an airtight lid and heat in a water bath at 80°C / 170°F for 30 minutes.

Tighten lid and store.

The sauce will store for several months and should be kept in a fridge once opened.

TOMATO JUICE

Extract the juice using a fruit press or electric juicer. Freshly-pressed juice will keep only for a day or two in the fridge – but don't forget to freeze some. This can be done in plastic bags inside small boxes (e.g. juice cartons) – when frozen the boxes can be removed and the blocks of juice packed together. Empty plastic milk cartons can also be used for freezing juice – but they must be thoroughly cleaned, and don't forget to leave 5cm / 2 inches space for expansion as the juice freezes.

■ ■ ■

TURNIPS

There are several different varieties of turnips which can be harvested throughout most times of the year. Like radishes, the roots are only half submerged in the soil and, can be left there until required. They are not fully frost-hardy, however, so should be lifted and stored before the depths of winter. To avoid woodiness, the roots should be pulled before they reach tennis-ball size. Harvested turnips will keep fresh in the fridge for several weeks.

Recommended varieties

Purple Top Milan (quick to mature. Sow in March for an early crop)
White Globe (smooth roots with white tender flesh)
Golden Ball (round golden roots with yellow flesh, stores well)

Freeze

Wash, trim and cut into chunks before blanching for 3 minutes. Freeze in plastic bags. To cook from frozen, boil for about 8 minutes.

Dry storage

Pull up in November and gently remove the soil from undamaged roots. Twist off the foliage and pack the roots in sand in boxes – store in a cool, frost-free building.

Clamp

Can be a useful temporary technique for larger quantities. See 'Clamping' in Part One (pages 15-16) for details.

Index

Items in *italic* are recipes.

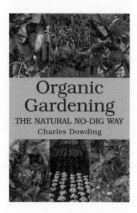
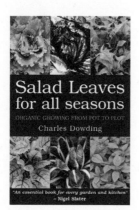